Cronin

IRISH FREEDOM PRESS – CLÓ SAOIRSE

223 Parnell Street, Dublin 1, Ireland.

Tel: (01) 8729747 Fax: (01) 8729757

e-mail: saoirse@iol.ie

Acknowledgements

In preparing this short study of the Easter Rising, I read a great deal of contemporary material. The Castle view of the Insurrection is based on the minutes of evidence and report of "The Royal Commission on the Irish Rebellion, 1916" which is available in the New York Public Library.

I acknowledge gratefully the assistance of Brian Murphy who designed the cover and with Deasún Breatnach saw the manuscript through the Printers; Risteárd de Róiste, who interviewed the 1916 veteran, Joseph Clarke; Jim O'Connor, editor of "The Advocate", New York, for the use of his files; Easter Week survivors Sam O'Reilly, Jim Mooney and the late Tom Dunne whose stories I first told in "The Advocate" in April-May, 1951, and recall briefly here.

I also wish to thank the following: The Yeats family and the Macmillan Company, for extracts from the poems of W. B. Yeats; the Irish Transport and General Workers' Union, for quotations from the writings of James Connolly; Miss Margaret Pearse and the Talbot Tress, for quotations from "The Collected Works of P. H. Pearse"; An tOllamh Liam O Briain and C. J. Fallon, Ltd., for the former's reminiscences in "Ireland – 1851-1921" (edited by James Carty); the Editor, the "Irish Times", for extracts from "Weekly Irish Times Handbook of the Sinn Féin Rebellion (1916)"; Padraic Colum, for Mary M. Colum's memory of Pearse from "The Irish Rebellion of 1916 and Its Martyrs", published in New York in 1916 by Devin-Adair Co., edited by Maurice Joy; the MacDonagh and Plunkett families for poems of the leaders.

I have indicated throughout the text the source of other quotations. Works I found useful included R. M. Henry's "Sinn Féin", Desmond Ryan's "The Rising", James Stephens' "The Insurrection in Dublin", "The Shaping of Modern Ireland", edited by Conor Cruise O'Brien. For any omissions from this list, my apologies.

SEÁN CRONIN.

New York.
February, 1966.

Preface

This short book was first published in 1966 for the fiftieth anniversary of the Easter Rising, a time when the merits of that dramatic event were less subject to controversy than now. But then the Rising itself was hardly a popular event when it occurred. This work examines how Dublin Castle saw, or did not see, the Rising unfold. Behind all that one must constantly keep in mind the statement of Augustine Birrell, the British Chief Secretary in 1916, that "nobody in Ireland, North or South, save a handful of officials was, or ever had been, loyal to England in the true sense of the word."

This edition is slightly revised. The changes are minor: correction of typographical errors, a couple of misplaced paragraphs have been put in their proper order, some material on the Rising in Co. Galway has been added. Essentially the two editions are the same.

I would like to thank Seán Ó Brádaigh for his help in seeing this edition through the press. He displayed his usual patience, courtesy and competence in doing so.

SEÁN CRONIN

New York
August, 1976

I am pleased that Irish Freedom Press will publish a third edition of *Our Own Red Blood* this year, the ninetieth anniversary of the Easter Rising. The idealism and courage of the men and women of 1916 will always inspire freedom-loving people, both in Ireland and throughout the world.

SEÁN CRONIN

Washington
January, 2006

Our Own Red Blood

"But where can we draw water?"
Said Pearse to Connolly,
"When all the wells are parched away?
O plain as plain can be
There's nothing but our own red blood
Can make a right rose tree."

– W. B. Yeats.

PART ONE

Tuesday, May 2, 1916.

In a room at Richmond Barracks, Dublin, a field court-martial convenes. The beribboned officers range in rank from lieutenant to brigadier. Military and Dublin Castle detectives pack the small court area. Standing at the back, surrounded by guards, is the prisoner, a tall, well-built man in the green homespun uniform of the Irish Volunteers. He wears neither badges nor decorations. His pale face is composed.

The prisoner's name is Patrick Henry Pearse. His crime is "rebellion with the intent of assisting the enemy." Britain is at war and her enemy is Germany. A rebellion has been crushed in Dublin. The prisoner led it.

The proceedings are brief. There is no defence counsel. There is no defence. Pearse is identified as a member of the rebel forces by British military held prisoner in the General Post Office during the Rising. Detectives give evidence of "political character," describing Pearse as a leading figure in such seditious bodies as the Irish Volunteers and the Irish Republican Brotherhood.

The president of the court puts a question. The prisoner replies with a short statement.

No records are available of the secret tribunal. The statement came to light thirty years after the trial when the relatives of a dead British sergeant, who had been stationed in Kilmainham Prison during the Rising, handed it to the Pearse family. In a covering note, dated May 2, 1916, Pearse called the speech "the substance of what I said when asked today by the president of the court-martial at Richmond Barracks whether I had anything to say in my defence."

Here it is in full:

> I desire, in the first place, to repeat what I have already said in letters to General Maxwell and Brigadier-General Lowe. My object in agreeing to an unconditional surrender was to prevent the further slaughter of the civil population of Dublin and to save the lives of our gallant followers, who, having made for six days a stand unparalleled in military history, were now surrounded and in the case of those under the immediate command of headquarters without food. I fully understand now, as then, that my own life is forfeit to British law, and I shall die very cheerfully if I can think that the British Government, as it has already shown itself strong. will now show itself magnanimous enough to accept my single life in forfeiture and to give a general amnesty to the brave men and boys who have fought at my bidding.

> In the second place, I wish it to be understood that any admissions I make here are to be taken as involving myself alone. They

do not involve and must not be used against anyone who acted with me, not even those who may set their names to documents with me.

I admit that I was Commandant-General commanding-in-chief the forces of the Irish Republic which have been acting against you for the past week, and that I was President of the Provisional Government. I stand over all my acts and words done or spoken in these capacities. When I was a child of ten I went down on my bare knees by my bedside one night and promised God that I should devote my life to an effort to free my country. I have kept the promise. As a boy and as a man I have worked for Irish freedom, first among all earthly things. I have helped to organise, to arm, to train, and to discipline my fellow-countrymen to the sole end that, when the time came, they might fight for Irish freedom. The time, as it seemed to me, did come, and we went into the fight. I am glad we did; we seem to have lost, but we have not lost. To refuse to fight would have been to lose, to fight is to win; we have kept faith with the past and handed on a tradition to the future.

I repudiate the assertion of the prosecutor that I sought to aid and abet England's enemy. Germany is no more to me than England is. I asked and accepted German aid in the shape of arms and an expeditionary force; we neither asked for nor accepted German gold, nor had any traffic with Germany but what I state. My aim was to win Irish freedom. We struck the first blow ourselves, but I should have been glad of an ally's aid.

I assume that I am speaking to Englishmen who value their freedom and who profess to be fighting for the freedom of Belgium and Serbia; believe that we, too, love freedom and desire it. To us it is more desirable than anything in the world. If you strike us down now we shall rise again and renew the fight; you cannot conquer Ireland, you cannot extinguish the Irish passion for freedom; if our deed has not been sufficient to win freedom then our children will win it by a better deed.

The trial ends. Pearse is taken to the barrack gymnasium to await the conclusion of other trials. Among the defendants that day are two signatories of the Proclamation of the Irish Republic, Thomas J. Clarke and Thomas MacDonagh.

(2)

Tom Clarke in 1916 was a greyhaired man of 58 with a thin, worn face and wiry body. He was born in the Isle of Wight where his father, a Co. Leitrim man, was stationed as a sergeant in the British Army. Later they moved to Dungannon. In 1881, already a member of the I.R.B., Clarke emigrated to America. Two years later he volunteered for the dynamite campaign in England which one wing of the Clan na Gael – the Triangle led by Alexander Sullivan – had organised despite the opposition of such Fenian leaders as John Devoy in America, James Stephens in France and John O'Leary in Ireland. British espionage was effective; Tom Clarke was quickly arrested, tried and sentenced to penal servitude for life under the name Henry Hammond Wilson. He spent more than fifteen years in various British jails.

The campaign was bloodless except for the death of the '67 Fenian leader, William Mackey Lomasney (the "Little Captain"), killed in 1884 trying to blow up London Bridge. Explosions occurred in the Houses of Parliament and other public buildings, but no lives were lost. Nevertheless, the twenty-five men sentenced to long prison sentences in connection with the dynamitings received brutal treatment. Two of Clarke's comrades, Dr. Gallagher and Alfred Whitehead lost their reason. At one time Tom Clarke feared for his own sanity. His *Glimpses of an Irish Felon's Prison Life* tells in unadorned prose the story of his prolonged captivity.

During the Parnell Commission hearings* a Scotland Yard inspector offered Tom Clarke freedom and a civil service job if he would testify for the crown. They wanted him to say the Irish leader controlled the revolutionary movement. "I'd prefer to stay here till the day of judgment," Tom Clarke replied.

He was released in 1898 and sailed for America a year later. John Devoy was in charge of the Clan na Gael and Tom Clarke went to work for him. When the *Gaelic-American* was founded in 1903, Clarke became its bookkeeper. He married Kathleen Daly, daughter of fellow-felon John Daly of Limerick, and farmed for a time at Manorville, Long Island. But Ireland kept calling and in 1908 he returned with his family.

They settled in Dublin. Clarke bought a tobacconist shop first in Amiens Street and then in Parnell Street and they became meeting places for the young men with advanced ideas. Tom was a taciturn man who listened far more than he talked. It was a time of national awakening; the language revival, the literary renaissance, Alice Milligan's *Shan Van Vocht,* Arthur Griffith's *United Irishman,* the study of Republican ideas following the '98 centenary, combined to create a new atmosphere which exhilarated the young. In 1905 Sinn Féin was founded. Three years later it fought a by-election in Leitrim when the Home Rule member, C. J. Dolan, resigned his seat to join the new movement and then sought it back. Although Sinn Féin put up a good fight, Dolan was beaten. But it was the first challenge parliamentarianism had received in a long time.

---

* Special Commission set up by British Government following series in *The Times* (London) in 1887 called "Parnellism and Crime". Richard Pigott sold forged letters to *The Times* for £1,780 and they published some of them. A British agent in the Clan na Gael named Le Caron gave evidence at the hearings. *The Times* lost, Pigott shot himself, and Parnell's prestige in Ireland was higher than ever.

Castle detectives watched Clark's movements; Post Office censors read his mail. The authorities listed him as "dangerously seditious" and those who visited him were put in the same category.

Many of the latter belonged to the I.R.B. Clarke found the revolutionary organisation moribund. Its ageing leaders mistook talk for activity. Clarke rallied the younger element and built up a team of ardent young organisers, like Seán Mac Diarmada, who moved about the country spreading the separatist doctrine of Tone. Within a few years the reinvigorated I.R.B. launched the monthly *Irish Freedom*. By 1912 control of the organisation was in the hands of Tom Clarke and his young allies. When World War I began they pushed through a resolution urging insurrection.

Tom Clarke's name tops the others in the Proclamation, an honour accorded him by the Military Council because of his long service to Ireland. There is no record of what he said at the court-martial, or if he spoke at all. He was no speech-maker. But he did tell his wife before the end: "I'm glad it's to be the firing squad. I've had enough of imprisonment". And he assured her that 1916 was the start of a new phase in the fight for freedom, not – as so often in Irish history – the depressing end of another defeated rising.

On the surface Thomas MacDonagh was as unlike Tom Clarke as two men could be: he was assistant professor of English at University College Dublin, a critic of distinction, a poet of promise, commandant of the Dublin Brigade, Irish Volunteers and 38 years of age in 1916. Like Clarke, what moved him was the dynamic of Irish nationalism. Like his mentor Pearse, MacDonagh's road to the firing squad lay through the language revival movement. "The Gaelic revival has given to some of us a new arrogance," he wrote once. "I am a Gael and I know no cause but of pride in that – *Gaedheal mé agus ní heol dom gur náir dom é.*"

Thomas MacDonagh was a short intense man with a flow of "learned, witty and humorous talk", according to his friend, the poet Padraic Colum. He came from Cloughjordan, Co. Tipperary, the child of school teachers. He loved books and developed a feeling for words. He was a scholastic at Rockwell College, Cashel, for a time, discovered he had no vocation and went on to the National University. He studied in Paris, wrote a play called "When the Dawn is Come" which the Abbey produced in 1907, published some books of verse and a critical study, *Literature in Ireland*. When Pearse founded St. Enda's he chose MacDonagh as his first master. Around 1911 MacDonagh joined Joseph Plunkett in editing *Irish Review* and immersed himself in national affairs.*

---

* *Irish Review* was a monthly founded by Professor David Houston of the College of Science. Thomas MacDonagh, Padraic Colum, James Stephens, George Moore, AE and Pearse wrote for it. Joseph Plunkett took it over in the Spring of 1913. Ten more numbers were issued before it was suppressed in November, 1914.

According to his own account, MacDonagh's trial lasted fifteen minutes. His final statement was taken down by an officer with shorthand and someone got it and had it printed. Newsboys distributed it in the streets and the military raided the printing house. Some doubts have been cast on its authenticity but certain passages have MacDonagh's unmistakable stamp. One runs:

> While Ireland lives, the brains and brawn of her manhood will strive to destroy the last vestige of British rule in her territory. In this ceaseless struggle there will be, as there has been, and must be, an alternate ebb and flow. But let England make no mistake. The generous high-bred youth of Ireland will never fail to answer the call we pass on – will never fail to blaze forth in the red rage of war to win their country's freedom. Other and tamer methods they will leave to other and tamer men; but they must do or die.

Sometime around midnight of May 2, Pearse, Clarke and MacDonagh learned they were to be shot at dawn. And they were.

(3)

Pádraic Pearse spent his last hours composing a letter and finishing two poems, "The Wayfarer" and "The Mother". In the letter he said:

"We have done right. People will say hard things of us now, but later on will praise us".

The letter was to his mother. Margaret Brady was a Dublin woman who married an English sculptor named James Pearse. When her sons went out to fight she was a widow. Pearse captures her strength and nobility in that last poem where he has her say:

> I do not grudge them; Lord, I do not grudge
> My two strong sons that I have seen go out
> To break their strength and die, they and a few,
> In bloody protest for a glorious thing.
> They shall be spoken of among their people,
> The generations shall remember them,
> And call them blessed...

Pearse was a product of the Gaelic League, the language revival movement which inspired many of the literary and political ideas that outraged Victorian Dublin at the turn of the century. Dr. Douglas Hyde founded the League in 1893. He began his crusade with the now famous lecture "The Necessity for deAnglicising Ireland"* which ends

* Delivered to the Irish National and Literary Society in Dublin, November 25, 1892. The Society was the precursor of the dramatic movement which culminated in the foundation of the Abbey Theatre.

with the plea: "In order to de-anglicise ourselves we must at once arrest the decay of the language." His words became the watchword of a generation.

"What the battleaxe of the Dane, the sword of the Norman, the wile of the Saxon were unable to perform, we have accomplished ourselves", said Hyde. "We have at last broken the continuity of Irish life . . .

"Just when we should be starting to build up anew the Irish race and the Gaelic nation – as within our own recollection Greece has been built up anew – we find ourselves despoiled of the bricks of nationality. The old bricks that lasted eighteen hundred years are destroyed; we must now set to, to bake new ones, if we can, on other ground and of other clay. Imagine for the moment the restoration of a German-speaking Greece."

This was inconceivable. The birthright cast aside must be recovered. Catholics and Protestants, Nationalists and Unionists flocked to learn Irish in the League's draughty halls, and mounted platforms to urge everyone to speak the language, sing the songs and dance the dances of the Gael. Pearse joined at 16. Dr. Hyde's "Abhráin Ghrádha Chúige Chonnacht" (The Love Songs of Connacht) influenced Yeats, Synge and Lady Gregory. But they wrote in English. Its effect on Pearse was to send him to Rosmuc in Connemara summer after summer until he became fluent in the language. Then poems, stories, plays – all in Irish – flowed from his pen.

Pádraic Pearse was a graduate of the Royal University and a barrister. He preferred journalism to law and became editor of *An Claidheamh Soluis,* the Gaelic League's bilingual organ. A man of enormous energy, he felt too little was being done to arrest the anglicising process, especially in the secondary schools where education was patterned on English lines. He decided to found a school based on national ideas and went to Belgium and Holland to study bilingual methods of teaching.

St. Enda's began in September 1908. Named for the 5th century Aran scholar who founded the first of the great Celtic Christian schools, the difficulties the venture faced were enormous, and lack of money was only one. The idea of a lay boarding school for boys met strong opposition, Irish secondary education being almost exclusively in the hands of religious orders. Pearse was a determined man. Aided by Thomas MacDonagh, his brother Willie Pearse, his mother – she managed the domestic side of St. Enda's – he broke down prejudices and overcame obstacles. St. Enda's first location was Cullenswood House, Ranelagh. Two years later the school was transferred to The Hermitage, Rathfarnham, and Cullenswood House became the girls' school, St. Ita's.

A fresco in the entrance hall of St. Enda's depicted the boy hero Cú Chulainn taking arms for the first time. A druid tells him he will have a short life, but a glorious one. Cú Chulainn's reply, inscribed in Old Irish, ran: "I care not if my life have only the span of a night and a day if my deeds be spoken of by the men of Ireland."

Pearse was an innovator, in education as in so many other things. The country's foremost intellects lectured to the boys. He wrote plays which the students produced and acted. Perhaps the following extract from the school magazine, *An Macaomh*, for Christmas 1909, explains best what Pádraic Pearse had in mind for St. Enda's:

> In truth, I think, that the old Irish plan of education, as idealised for boys in the story of the Macradh of Eamhain and for girls in that of the Grianán of Lusga, was the wisest and most generous that the world has ever known. The bringing together of children in some pleasant place under the fosterage of some man famous among his people for his greatness of heart, for his wisdom, for his skill in some gracious craft – here we get the two things on which I lay most stress in education, the environment, and the stimulus of a personality which can address itself to the child's worthiest self. Then, the character of free government, within certain limits, the right to make laws and maintain them, to elect and depose leaders – here was scope for the growth of individualities yet provision for maintaining the suzerainty of the common weal; the scrupulous co-relation of moral, intellectual and physical training, the open-air life, the very type of the games which formed so large a part of their learning – all these things were designed with a largeness of view foreign to the little minds that devise our modern makeshifts for education. Lastly, the "aite", fosterer or teacher, had as colleagues in his work of fosterage no ordinary hirelings, but men whom their gifts of soul, or mind, or body, had lifted high above their contemporaries – the captains, the poets, the prophets of the people.

Mary Colum, writer-wife of Padraic Colum, taught at St. Ita's for a time. She knew Pearse well. She describes him as follows:

> In conversation he was gentle and shy, only in the presence of large masses of people did he really become himself. Then he became imperious and masterful and his strength and passion were sometimes overwhelming. He was the finest orator I have ever heard, though his oratory was not of the kind common amongst the Irish members of the House of Commons and in many Irish-American gatherings, and which is known as *raiméis* in Ireland. Everything Pearse said was charged with meaning, and took root in the heads and hearts of the people. He never worked up his audience into tears about the past woes of Ireland; he made them passionately eager to struggle for the future. Thus, he dominated that generation of university-bred men and women in Ireland who have risked so much and accomplished so much. I can easily

understand how, when the choice of President of the Republic had to be taken, all minds and eyes turned to him.*

Pearse did not jump hastily into revolutionary politics. He was 34 when he joined the I.R.B. in the summer of 1913. He had lost faith in Home Rule as a stepping stone to independence. The Gaelic League, he felt, was a spent force. In "The Coming Revolution" (Nov.1913) he explains what he meant by describing the Gaelic League as a spent force. "I mean that the vital work to be done in the new Ireland will be done not so much by the Gaelic League itself as by men and movements that have sprung from the Gaelic League or have received from the Gaelic League a new baptism and a new life of grace."

He tells his fellow-Gaelic Leaguers: "As to what your work as an Irish Nationalist is to be, I cannot conjecture; I know what mine is to be, and would have you know yours and buckle yourselves to it. And it may be (nay, it is) that yours and mine will lead us to a common meeting-place, and that on a certain day we shall stand together, with many more beside us, ready for a greater adventure than any of us has yet had, a trial and a triumph to be endured and achieved in common."

But he notes too an important spiritual change in Irish separatism:

"A new junction has been made with the past; into the movement that has never wholly died since '67, have come the young men of the Gaelic League."

In November 1913 the Irish Volunteers were formed. What began as a response to Carson's Ulster Volunteers generated great national enthusiasm and although planned as a broad movement embracing Redmond's parliamentary party, Griffith's Sinn Féin, Republicans and men of no particular political affiliation it soon became evident that the I.R.B. held a key role in the organisation. Eoin MacNeill, a co-founder of the Gaelic League and professor of Celtic Studies at U.C.D. was named President and later Chief-of-Staff. His article "The North Began", suggesting that the rest of Ireland follow Ulster's example, began the train of events which led to the meeting in the Rotunda on November 25, 1913. Pearse later became Director of Organisation.¶ Others influential in the Volunteers were Bulmer Hobson, a Protestant I.R.B. man from Belfast who was close to MacNeill, Roger Casement, The O'Rahilly and Colonel Maurice Moore.

"We have started an insurrection," Pearse told a companion as they left the Rotunda. Having ignored the Ulster Volunteers, the British

* "The Irish Rebellion of 1916" edited by Maurice Joy, New York, 1916.

¶ On December 6, 1914, at the first convention of the Volunteers after the split with Redmond.

government could do nothing. John Redmond feared his "national authority" might be circumvented and decided to control the new movement. Despite opposition from the I.R.B., the Volunteer Executive agreed to share leadership with Redmond and a joint committee was set up. Hobson favoured this division of authority, breaking with his I.R.B. comrades on the issue. Pearse opposed it with the warning:

> The leaders in Ireland have nearly always left the people at the critical moment; they have sometimes sold them. The former Volunteer movement was abandoned by its leaders; O'Connell recoiled before the cannon at Clontarf; twice the hour of the Irish revolution struck during Young Ireland days and twice it struck in vain, for Meagher hesitated in Waterford, Duffy and McGee hesitated in Dublin. Stephens refused to give the word in '65; he never came in '66 or '67. I do not blame these men; you or I might have done the same. It is a terrible responsibility to be cast on a man, that of bidding the cannon speak and the grapeshot pour.

As the political pace quickened, Pearse became the voice of the Republicanism and the conscience of the militant Irish-Irelanders. "We have come to the holiest place in Ireland," he told the 1913 Wolfe Tone commemoration in Bodenstown. "Holier to us than the place where Patrick sleeps in Down. Patrick brought us life, but this man died for us." In New York the following year, he addressed Emmet commemorations in Manhattan and Brooklyn, and met John Devoy. The Rising began to take shape in his mind and the Emmet model probably played a part in his thinking.

Pearse's social ideas matured rapidly too, especially under the impact of the 1913 Dublin strike. By 1915, when he wrote *The Sovereign People,* he had reached conclusions close to those of James Connolly on the political, economic, and social implications of freedom. His approach was different. Like Connolly he was influenced by the essays of James Fintan Lalor.

Meantime, war engulfed country after country; yet no submerged small nation rose to claim its freedom. That honour was reserved for Ireland. The idea of blood sacrifice as the only means open to independence – the dramatic deed rather than the sacred word – took possession of Pearse. "There are many things more horrible than bloodshed," he wrote, "and slavery is one of them." In August, 1915, he put that view another way at the grave of O'Donovan Rossa*:

> Life springs from death; and from the graves of patriot men and women spring living nations. The defenders of this realm have

* Jeremiah O'Donovan Rossa (1831-1915), Fenian leader, sentenced to life imprisonment in 1865, released 1871, went into exile in America where he died 44 years later.

worked well in secret and in the open. They think that they have pacified Ireland. They think that they have purchased half of us and intimidated the other half. They think that they have foreseen everything, think that they have provided against everything: but the fools, the fools, the fools! – they have left us our Fenian dead, and while Ireland holds these graves, Ireland unfree shall never be at peace.

Pearse spoke in low tones, his hearers attested. When be had finished, round after round of cheering broke the silence of Glasnevin cemetery. Such words were new in Ireland.

Also new was his vision of the Ireland he hoped would follow. "The clear true eyes of this man, almost alone in his day, visioned Ireland as we of today would surely have her: *not free merely, but Gaelic as well; not Gaelic merely, but free as well,*" he declared of Rossa. The ideology of the Gaelic League was to provide the mortar of the New Ireland.

(4)

Late on May 2, British military fetched relatives of the condemned men and drove them through the dark, scarred streets of Dublin to Kilmainham Prison.

Kathleen Clarke, herself a prisoner, found her husband in good cheer. The visit was brief. Afterwards he wrote a short note which she received next day when he was dead. "Make no mistake about it," the old rebel declared, "freedom is coming, but not all at once. There will be another big fight. We all believe this and in that we die happy."

Thomas MacDonagh's wife could not make the journey; his sister, a nun, took her place. She found the cell lighted by a guttering candle. When she asked a soldier for water so that her brother might wash, she received the curt reply, "No".

Later he wrote his wife: "I counted the cost of this, and I am ready to pay it". He had already composed his epitaph.

> His songs were a little phrase
> Of eternal song.
> Drowned in the harping lays
> More loud and long.

> His deed was a single word
> Called out alone
> In a night where no echo stirred
> To laughter or moan.

But his songs new souls shall thrill
The loud harps dumb,
And his deed the echoes fill
When the dawn is come.

Louis Le Roux* says Willie Pearse was brought from his cell, possibly to bid his brother goodbye. Whatever the intention it came to nothing; as he moved down a corridor under escort an officer shouted:

"Take him back. Too late. Too late". Then they heard shots.

It was bitterly cold at 3.30 a.m. even in May. Each prisoner had his hands tied behind his back, a cloth placed over his eyes, a small piece of white paper about five inches square pinned to his coat over the heart. They died singly in the jail yard, their backs to the wall. The volleys followed one another quickly.

The bodies were thrown into an army wagon, covered with blankets, carted across the city to Arbour Hill Barracks, cast into prepared graves, sprinkled with quicklime and covered with clay. Tom Clarke first, Thomas MacDonagh next, and then Pádraic Pearse. An N.C.O. checked the details for army files.

Some hours later the military authorities announced the trials and executions of May 3.

(5)

Thursday, May 4, 1916.

British military headquarters announces the executions of Joseph Plunkett, Edward Daly, Michael O'Hanrahan, William Pearse following trial by field court-martial.

Joseph Mary Plunkett eldest son of George Noble Count Plunkett, fought in the G.P.O. with his brothers George and Jack, and distinguished himself during the evacuation by rallying the Volunteers under the crossfire of Moore Street. Despite poor health, he played a man's part in the cause of Ireland.

A student of military tactics, Plunkett is credited with drafting the general plan of the Rising. Late in 1915 he went to Germany as envoy of the I.R.B., travelling through Spain, Italy and Switzerland. From Berne he sent a message to Roger Casement then in Germany. He returned to Ireland by way of New York.

Joseph Plunkett was a poet and close friend of Thomas MacDonagh. He wrote for *Irish Freedom* and *Irish Review*, which he also edited. In 1913 he published *The Circle and The Sword*, a book of verse. One poem runs:

* *The Man Called Pearse* by Louis Le Roux.

17

All our best ye have branded
When the people were choosing them,
When 'twas death they demanded,
Ye laughed! Ye were losing them!
But the blood that ye spilt in the night
Crieth loudly to God,
And their name hath the strength and the might
Of a sword from the sod.

Another called "The Heritage" opens thus:

The hand that fought, the hearts that broke
In old immortal tragedies,
These have not failed beneath the skies,
Their children's heads refuse the yoke.

This heritage to the race of kings:
Their children and their children's seed
Have wrought their prophecies in deed
Of terrible and splendid things.

Plunkett married Grace Gifford, his fiancee, shortly before his execution. Armed troops filled the small candle-lit chapel; a British soldier stood witness. The couple were together for a few minutes after the ceremony; then she was led from the prison and he was led to his death. At 29, Joseph Plunkett was the youngest of the seven signatories of the Proclamation.

Edward Daly was a brother of Kathleen Clarke; he commanded the First Battalion in the Four Courts and North King Street area. Nurse Elizabeth O'Farrell relates that "he was very much cut up about the surrender but accepted his orders as a soldier should". Michael O'Hanrahan was a writer and Irish language revivalist; he was with MacDonagh at Jacob's factory. Willie Pearse, a sculptor like his father, was in the G.P.O.; but he was not a leading figure either before or during the Rising. He was executed because his name was Pearse.

Friday, May 5, 1916.

The British announce the execution of John MacBride.

Major MacBride, a native of Mayo, commanded the Irish Brigade against the British in the Boer War. He joined MacDonagh's command on the morning of the Rising. He refused a blindfold, facing the firing squad with the quip: "I have looked down the barrels of their rifles before".

Monday, May 8, 1916.

Executions announced of Eamonn Ceannt, Michael Mallin, Seán Heuston, Con Colbert.

Ceannt, a member of Sinn Féin and a founder-member of the Volunteers, came to separatism through the Gaelic League. He was officer commanding the 4th Battalion, Dublin Brigade. During the Rising he commanded the South Dublin Union garrison where his second in command was the heroic Cathal Brugha. Ceannt was a big man; a contemporary news report describes his bearing at the surrender as "noble almost magnificent". He was a signatory of the Proclamation.

On Sunday afternoon, May 7, Ceannt learned he was to die in the morning. He wrote letters to his wife and son and drafted a brief message to his countrymen in which he paid this tribute to the men who fought with him: "All were simply splendid. Even I knew no fear or panic, and shrank from no risk, even as I shrink not now from the death which faces me at daybreak".

Michael Mallin was Chief of Staff of the Citizen Army under James Connolly, and commanded the main body of that force in St Stephen s Green during the Rising. Countess Markievicz was his second in command.

Seán Heuston and Con Colbert were Fianna leaders.* Despite their youth, they had long service in the national movement, belonging also to the I.R.B. and the Volunteers. Connolly told Heuston to hold the Mendicity Institute for three or four hours; he held it for four days. In his last letter to his sister he wrote: "Let there be no talk of 'foolish enterprises'. I have no vain regrets. If you really love me, teach the children the history of their own land, and teach them the cause of Caitlín Ní Uallacháin never dies. Ireland shall be free from the centre to the sea, as soon as the people of Ireland believe in the necessity of Ireland's freedom, and are prepared to make the necessary sacrifices to obtain it".

The soldier who pinned the white paper on Colbert's breast, shook the prisoner's hand warmly, Fr. Augustine, the Capuchin chaplain, relates, then bound his hands behind his back and blindfolded him. Colbert, who once refused a job with the British Civil Service after passing the examination because it involved taking an oath of allegiance to the Crown, was the kind of man who is admired even by his enemies.

Tuesday, May 9, 1916.

Thomas Kent is executed in Cork.

The Kents were prominent locally in national matters from Land

---

* Na Fianna Eireann, National Boy Scouts, founded by Countess Markievicz in 1909 as a Republican training corps for the youth of Ireland. Among the Fianna boys who achieved national prominence were Seán Heuston, Con Colbert and Liam Mellows.

League days. Thomas was prosecuted with Terence MacSwiney in 1915 for a seditious speech; Dublin Castle was furious when he went free and MacSwiney was fined only a shilling. So he was a target for the big round-up that followed the Rising. R.I.C. and military swooped on the Kent family home, Bawnard House, near Kanturk, on May 1, and met fierce resistance. Mrs. Kent, who was over 80, loaded the guns for her four sons. Richard Kent was killed, his brother David severely wounded. An R.I.C. officer also died in the fray. The surviving brothers were tried on a capital charge; David and Thomas were sentenced to death; William, the youngest, was acquitted. David was reprieved, and Thomas went to his death alone in Cork jail.

The executions shocked Ireland and dismayed friends of Ireland. On May 10 the influential liberal newspaper, the *Manchester Guardian,* called for an end to the shootings in Dublin. "It is monstrous that a military tribunal sitting in secret should be allowed to determine this great and critical matter in hot blood", said the *Guardian.* "The responsibility is for the Cabinet". The *New York Times* called the executions "incredible stupidity". Prime Minister H. H. Asquith visited Ireland and promised to stop the bloodletting. Connolly and MacDiarmada were still alive. On May 10, the *Irish Independent,* carried a photograph of Connolly over the lines: "Still lies in Dublin Castle slowly recovering from his wounds". An editorial declared:

> If these men are treated with too great leniency they will take it as an indication of weakness on the part of the Government; and the consequences may not be satisfactory. They may be more truculent than ever, and it is therefore necessary that society should be protected against their activity. Some of the leaders are more guilty and played a more sinister part in the campaign than those who have been already punished severely, and it would be hardly fair to treat these leniently because the cry for clemency has been raised, while those no more guilty than they have been severely punished. Weakness to such men at this stage may be fatal.

MacDiarmada and Connolly were put to death in the early hours of May 12.

(6)

Sean MacDiarmada was born near Kiltyclogher in North Leitrim. It is ruggedly beautiful country of mountains, bogs and lakes where the Gael survived the centuries of persecution and travail. The farms are small, the soil poor. The young emigrate when old enough to earn a living in some other country. Sean MacDiarmada left home at fifteen, for Glasgow. During the next half dozen years be worked at a variety of unskilled jobs.

But among the emigrants he learned about his native country and its distressful history and it put iron in his soul.

When he was twenty-one MacDiarmada returned to Ireland and went to work in Belfast. He joined the Dungannon Club, a Republican group founded by Denis MacCullough and Bulmer Hobson. A year later he took the I.R.B. oath and moved to Dublin, where his association with Tom Clarke began.

The I.R.B. was organised in circles. District and county representatives elected the Supreme Council of eleven. Seven of the eleven were provincial representatives – Ulster, Munster, Leinster, Connacht, South England, North England, Scotland – and four were co-opted. The president, secretary and treasurer of the Supreme Council formed the executive which controlled the organisation between meetings of the council.

MacDiarmada became a full-time organiser of the I.R.B. and Sinn Féin. He moved about the country on foot and on bicycle, and in scores of small towns and villages became known to separatists and to R.I.C. alike. The police entered him in their notebooks as "John MacDermott", and reported his movements to Dublin Castle.

When the I.R.B. launched *Irish Freedom* in the autumn of 1910 with the announced policy of "complete and total separation from England", MacDiarmada became the paper's manager. He had an office at 12 D'Olier Street, Dublin. He set up Wolfe Tone clubs which propagated the political philosophy of the founder of the United Irishmen and also sold the monthly *Irish Freedom*.

MacDiarmada was an organiser not a writer. It is doubtful if he wrote a line for *Irish Freedom*. But he inspired others. The paper laid down the guiderails of Irish nationalism. It blasted the sectarianism of the Parliamentary party under Redmond and Devlin. The following is a typical comment:

> This narrowing down of nationalism to the members of one creed is the most fatal thing that has taken place in Irish politics since the days of the Pope's Brass Band ... That the driving power of the official Nationalists should be supplied by an organisation (the A.O.H.) of which no Protestant, however good a patriot, can be a member, is in direct opposition to the policies and traditions of Irish Nationalism.

MacDiarmada was a founder-member of the Volunteers. By 1914 he was treasurer of the Supreme Council of the I.R.B. Tom Clarke was secretary. Together they pushed for the policy of insurrection which the Supreme Council adopted on September 5, 1914. The resolution was threefold: the I.R.B. would organise a rising if (1) the Germans invaded, (2) the British tried to enforce conscription, (3) the war seemed on the point of ending without a blow for Irish freedom. The resolution was affirmed at subsequent meetings of the Supreme Council, the last time early in 1916.

To prepare for the rising, the executive in May, 1915, set up a military sub-committee consisting of Clarke, MacDiarmada, Pearse and Plunkett. Later Eamonn Ceannt was added. James Connolly joined in January 1916 and Thomas MacDonagh joined in April.*

A new Supreme Council was elected in *September,* 1915, with Clarke, MacDiarmada, Pearse and Dr. Patrick McCartan as co-opted members; the provincial representatives were: Denis MacCullough (Ulster), Seán Tobin (Leinster), Diarmuid Lynch (Munster), Alastair MacCaba (Connacht), Richard Connolly (South England), Joseph Gleeson (North England) and Pat McCormack (Scotland). Denis MacCullough was president. Clarke and MacDiarmada were reaffirmed in their Executive posts of secretary and treasurer.

When the Supreme Council met again in December it approved the general plan for a rising. By then the Military Council had transformed itself into a revolutionary committee for mobilising and directing all militant national forces including the I.R.B., the Volunteers, Sinn Féin and the Citizen Army along insurrectionary lines. Its members signed the Proclamation of the Republic and formed the Provisional Government.

MacDiarmada was jailed for four months in 1915 for an anti-recruiting speech in Tuam, Co. Galway. He had confidential papers on him when arrested, but managed to smuggle them to Liam Mellows before the R.I.C. searched him.

During the Rising, he was in the General Post Office, his most important work behind him. Stricken by a polio attack in 1912, he walked with the aid of a cane. He agreed to the surrender to save Dublin from destruction. He told the Volunteers on the last morning of the resistance: "This week of Easter will be remembered, and your work will tell some day". In Richmond Barracks he remarked to fellow-prisoner Liam 0 Briain: "The only failure in Ireland is the failure to strike".

We have no record of what MacDiarmada said at his trial, or whether he spoke at all. On May 11, eve of execution, one of the Ryan sisters of Wexford visited him in Kilmainham. Later she wrote an account of it. He was lying on a plank bed in the tiny cell, still the same gay person everyone in the movement knew and loved. He said nothing about the court-martial, which was typical of him. She recalled that it rained that morning at 4 o'clock shortly after they shot Seán MacDiarmada at the age of 32.

(7)

James Connolly was a labour leader, a stocky man whose speech had a pronounced burr. He had lived and worked in Scotland, England, America and Ireland. People didn't trifle with him. He disliked

---

* This sub-committee became the military Council and took charge of the insurrection.

demagogues and those who prated about the beauties of Ireland. "Ireland without her people means nothing to me", he said once. He was an authority on Irish history, had schooled himself in economics, knew a number of languages and had a half-dozen trades. He was entirely self-taught. Life and the National Library were his universities.

Connolly was a pioneer. He preached industrial unionism when craft unionism was in the ascendancy. Events have proved Connolly right. His *Labour in Irish History* is a classic. An original work, it struck a new note. The way to plan a revolution he said, was to start first and get the guns afterward; provided conditions were ripe. This view scandalised MacNeill who thought Connolly impetuous. Connolly labelled MacNeill and his circle "legally seditious and peacefully revolutionary". Events unfortunately, proved him right here too.

Connolly's driving force was his passion for social justice. In 1896, in Dublin, he founded the Irish Socialist Republican Party. The name embodied his national, political and economic philosophy. The party had little success. In 1903 he emigrated to America and spent seven years there.

He returned to become Belfast district organiser of the Irish Transport and General Workers' Union under the dynamic Jim Larkin. Connolly's theories and Larkin's drive made the I.T.G.W.U. a force in Ireland. In a Belfast bitterly divided along religious lines Connolly told the workers: "I don't care where a man worships, but I do care where he gets his pay on a Saturday night". The object was One Big Union "with one card, one badge, one executive and one common enemy". Protestants and Catholics must stand together. One of Connolly's sayings was: "The only true prophets are they who carve out the future which they announce". Poorly paid unskilled labourers found spirit and militancy in the ranks of the I.T.G.W.U. and saw a new future opening up for themselves and their families and indeed Ireland as a whole.

The test came in Dublin in 1913. The four hundred employers of the capital, Unionist and Protestant for the most part, banded together under the leadership of another dynamic figure, William Martin Murphy, a Bantry-born Catholic Home Rule businessman who owned the Dublin Tramway Company and the daily *Irish Independent*. When the I.T.G.W.U. struck the trams during Horse Show Week, all the employers locked out the members of "Larkin's union" and soon 20,000 workers were walking the streets, jobless.

"Dublin is the most Christian city in these islands", said the writer George Russell (AE). "Its tottering tenements are holy". In 1913 a British Government inquiry found that 87,305 of Dublin's 400,000 people lived in the tottering tenements. "The sanitary conditions are revolting", said the *Irish Times*, commenting on the enquiry's findings. "Even the ordinary standards of savage morality can hardly be sustained".

The poor of Dublin were the worst housed and worst clad in Europe, with the possible exception of Naples. Women worked for five shillings a week; the average male wage ranged from fifteen to twenty-five shillings; skilled workers up to thirty-five shillings. Steady jobs were scarce. What the unskilled received depended on casual work. Unemployment was high.

The lock-out lasted six months. It was a massive effort to starve the poor into submission. English unions sent food; Irish emigrants sent money. Connolly and Larkin were jailed; Connolly went on hunger strike and the Viceroy freed him. Most workers stuck by their leaders. When it was all over Connolly paid this tribute to the women and men of Dublin:

> When that story (of the lock-out) is written by a man or woman with an honest heart, and with a sympathetic insight into the travail of the poor, it will be a record of which Ireland may well be proud.
>
> It will tell of how the old women and young girls, long crushed and enslaved, dared to risk all, even life itself, in the struggle to make life more tolerable, more free of the grinding tyranny of the soulless Dublin employers. It will tell of how, like an inspiration, there came to those Irish women and girls the thought that no free nation could be reared which tolerated the enslavement of its daughters to the worst forms of wage-slavery, and how in the glow of that inspiration they arose from their seats in the workshop or factory, and went out to suffer and struggle along with their men. It will tell of how the general labourers, the men upon whose crushed lives is built the fair fabric of civilisation, from whose squalid tenements the sweet-smelling flowers of capitalist culture derive their aroma, by whose horny hands and mangled bodies are bought the ease and safety of a class that hates and despises them, by whose ignorance their masters purchase their knowledge – it will tell how these labourers dared to straighten their bent backs, and looking in the faces of their rulers and employers, dared to express the will to be free. And it will tell how that spectacle of the slave of the underworld looking his masters in the face without terror, and fearlessly proclaiming the kinship and unity of all with each and each with all, how that spectacle caught the imagination of all unselfish souls so that the artisan took his place also in the place of conflict and danger, and the men and women of genius, the artistic and the literati, hastened to honour and serve those humble workers whom all had hitherto despised and scorned.

W. B. Yeats was one of the "men of genius" who spoke out for the workers of Dublin in their hour of need. He charged the Dublin Nationalist press "with deliberately arousing religious passion to break up the organisation of the working-man, with appealing to mob law day after day, with publishing the names of workingmen and their wives for purposes of intimidation". He charged the Dublin Unionist press with conniving at the conspiracy against the strikers. "Intriguers have met somewhere behind the scenes that they might turn the religion of Him who thought it hard for a rich man to enter into the Kingdom of Heaven into an oppression of the poor", his letter concluded.

With lacerating irony in the poem "September, 1913", he called Ireland's heroes as witnesses against the merchants of Dublin.

> What need you, being come to sense
> But fumble in a greasy till
> And add the halfpence to the pence
> And prayer to shivering prayer, until
> You have dried the marrow from the bone?
> For men were born to pray and save:
> Romantic Ireland's dead and gone,
> It's with O'Leary in the grave.
>
> Yet they were of a different kind,
> The names that stilled your childish play,
> They have gone about the world like wind,
> But little time had they to pray.
> For whom the hangman's rope was spun,
> And what, God help us. could they save?
> Romantic Ireland's dead and gone,
> It's with O'Leary in the grave.
>
> Was it for this the wild geese spread
> Their grey wing upon every tide;
> For this that all that blood was shed,
> For this Edward Fitzgerald died,
> And Robert Emmet and Wolfe Tone,
> All that delirium of the brave?
> Romantic Ireland's dead and gone,
> It's with O'Leary in the grave.

Pearse backed the strikers: "My instinct is with the landless man against the lord of lands. and with the breadless man against the master of millions. I may be wrong but I do hold it a most terrible sin that there should be landless men in this island of waste yet fertile valleys, and that there should be breadless men in this city where great fortunes are made and enjoyed". Tom Clarke protested the "inhuman savagery" of the police who batoned men, women and children on the streets. Joseph Plunkett and Thomas MacDonagh opened the columns of Irish Review to Connolly to state the workers' case.

Another writer, James Stephens, told the strikers: "You are as truly the liberators of the world today as were those twelve other workingmen who long ago threw up their jobs to follow the penniless Son of the Carpenter and your battle will not be a bit easier than theirs was". And George Russell in his letter "To the Masters of Dublin" said: "It remained for the twentieth century and the capital city of Ireland to see an oligarchy of four hundred masters deciding openly upon starving one hundred thousand people, and refusing to consider any solution except that fixed by their pride".

The Labour historian W. P. Ryan* writing of the 1913 struggle says Connolly "was a tower of strength in public and in private; in his addresses abroad, in his campaign directions, in his tactics in council. The spirit of the men, women and children in the dismal deeps of Dublin seemed to kindle his heart and give fire and inspiration to his utterances. The incoming of men and women, more socially favoured, to help in any and every fashion, from street corner speaking to cooking and serving in Liberty Hall and elsewhere, was a new feature in labour struggles in the capital. Francis Sheehy-Skeffington, his wife, and the Countess Markievicz were three out of many who threw themselves heart and soul into the work of feeding the spirits and the bodies of the locked-out wage-slaves and their families".

The employers hired strikebreakers and armed them. Dublin Castle permitted them to import weapons. The authorities crowded the jails with strikers. The law was on one side – the side of the masters. In self-defence, the workers established their own protective organisation and called it the Irish Citizen Army. "If it is right and legal for the men of Ulster to arm, then it is right and legal for the men of Dublin", thundered Larkin. Captain Jack White, a highly decorated ex-officer from the North, drilled the men and taught them the value of discipline when facing baton charges. Their only weapons were hurley sticks, but Labour was no longer defenceless.

The struggle ended in a stalemate. Larkin went to America in the autumn of 1914 and Connolly took over the leadership of the union and the Citizen Army. He also took over the *Irish Worker,* founded by Larkin in 1911 and which counted among its contributors, W. B. Yeats, James Stephens and Seán O'Casey. The Castle suppressed it under wartime powers. Connolly then founded *The Worker,* which he published in Glasgow. When that too was suppressed he established *The Workers' Republic,* printing it in Liberty Hall and setting the type by hand.

Liberty Hall, which the *Irish Times* was to call "the centre of social anarchy in Ireland, the brain of every riot and disturbance", was headquarters of the union and the Citizen Army. Called the Northumberland Buildings before 1912 when Larkin acquired it and gave it its new name, it had links with the independence struggle going back to 1848. When the war began Connolly draped a banner across the front with the slogan: "We Serve Neither King Nor Kaiser But Ireland". That was his view of the war.

* *The Irish Labour Movement* by W. P. Ryan, Dublin, 1919.

The pro-war sentiments of the labour leaders in Germany, France and Britain dismayed him; they out-jingoed the jingos. He had no illusion about war. "No, there is no such thing as a humane or civilised war", he wrote. "War may be forced upon a subject race or subject class to put an end to the subjection of race, or class or sex. When so waged it must be waged thoroughly and relentlessly, but with no delusions as to its elevating nature or civilising methods". He was not surprised when Britain used the pretext of the war to shelve Home Rule; Asquith's bill he considered "a pitiful abortion". He was among the first to see the evil of partition and warned labour to oppose the scheme to the death. As the war developed he leaned more and more towards a policy of armed resistance, building, training and arming the Citizen Army.

"We know our rulers", he wrote a friend in Scotland. "We know their power, and their ruthlessness we experience every day. We know they can force us to fight whether we wish to or not, but we also know that no force in their possession can decide for us *where* we will fight. That remains for us to decide; and we have no intention of shedding our blood abroad for our masters; rather we will elect to shed it if need be in the battle for the conquest of our *freedom at home*".

Connolly's frequent street manoeuvres alarmed Dublin Castle, the I.R.B. and the headquarters' staff of the Volunteers. At Christmas, 1915, Pearse told Desmond Ryan half-jokingly: "In private he (Connolly) says that the Germans are just as bad as the British, and that we ought to do the job ourselves ... He will never be satisfied until he goads us into action and then he will think most of us are too moderate, and want to guillotine half of us". He smiled, "I can see him setting up a guillotine, can't you? For Hobson and Mac Néill in particular. They are poles apart. What can he do anyway just now? Riot for a few days".*

Matters came to a head one month later. Connolly disappeared for three days; some thought the I.R.B. had kidnapped him. He was closeted with the Military Council and they reached agreement on a Rising. On January 22, 1916, *The Workers Republic* carried Connolly's provocative article, "What Is Our Programme?" The labour movement could not live on illusions, he wrote, but must build on the solid earth, unlike others who "spend their whole lives in following visions". From 1896, he continued, he had dedicated himself to the dictum that the freedom of Ireland should be secured "peacefully if possible, forcibly if necessary".

* Desmond Ryan, *The Rising*. The same author quotes Seán McGarry who as editor of the O'Donovan Rossa funeral souvenir asked Connolly for an article in July 1915 only to be told: "When are you fellows going to stop blethering about *dead* Fenians? Why don't you get a few live ones for a change?" But after a talk with Tom Clarke, Connolly wrote the article, "Why the Citizen Army honours Rossa".

"What is our programme now? At the grave risk of displeasing alike the perfervid Irish patriot and the British 'competent military authority', we shall tell it.

"We believe that in time of peace we should work along the lines of peace to strengthen the nation, and we believe that whatever strengthens and elevates the working class strengthens the nation.

"But we also believe that in times of war we should act as in war. We despise, entirely despise and loathe, all the mouthings and mouthers who infest Ireland in time of peace, just as we despise and loathe all the cantings about caution and restraint to which the same people treat us in times of war.

"Mark well then our programme. While the war lasts and Ireland still is a subject nation we shall continue to urge her to fight for her freedom.

"We shall continue, in season and out of season, to teach that the 'far-flung battle line' of England is weakest at the point nearest its heart, that Ireland is in that position of tactical advantage, that a defeat of England in India, Egypt, the Balkans or Flanders would not be so dangerous to the British Empire as any conflict of armed forces in Ireland, that the time for Ireland's battle is NOW, the place for Ireland's battle is HERE.

"That a strong man may deal lusty blows with his fists against a host of surrounding foes and conquer, but will succumb if a child sticks a pin in his heart.

"But the moment peace is once admitted by the British Government as being a subject ripe for discussion, *that moment our policy will be for peace* and in direct opposition to all talk or preparation for armed revolution.

"We will be no party to leading out Irish patriots to meet the might of an England at peace. The moment peace is in the air we shall strictly confine ourselves, and lend all our influence to the work of turning the thought of Labour in Ireland to the work of peaceful reconstruction.

"That is our programme. You can now compare it with the programme of those who bid you hold your hand now, and thus put it in the power of the enemy to patch up a temporary peace, turn round and smash you at his leisure, and then go to war again with the Irish question settled – in the graves of Irish patriots.

"We fear that is what is going to happen. It is to our mind inconceivable that the British public should allow conscription to be applied to England and not to Ireland. Nor do the British Government desire it. But that Government will use the cry of the necessities of war to force conscription upon the people of England, and will then make a temporary peace, and turn round to force Ireland to accept the same terms as have been forced upon England.

"The English public will gladly see this done – misfortune likes company. The situation will then shape itself thus : the Irish Volunteers who are pledged to fight conscription will either need to swallow their pledge, and see the young men of Ireland conscripted, or will need to resent conscription, and engage the military force of England at a time when England is at peace.

"This is what the diplomacy of England is working for, what the stupidity of some of our leaders who imagine they are Wolfe Tones is making possible. It is our duty, it is the duty of all who wish to save Ireland from such shame or such slaughter to strengthen the hand of those of the leaders who are for action as against those who are playing into the hands of the enemy.

"We are neither rash nor cowardly. We know our opportunity when we see it, and we know when it has gone. We know that at the end of this war England will have at least an army of one million men, or *more than two soldiers for every adult male in Ireland*. And these soldiers veterans of the greatest war in history.

"We shall not want to fight those men. We shall devote our attention to organising their comrades who return to civil life, to organising them into trade unions and Labour parties to secure them their rights in civil life.

"Unless we emigrate to some country where there are men.

"What Is Our Programme?" was a challenge to the leadership of the I.R.B. Connolly stated his position and wanted to know theirs. They told him during the "kidnapping" incident. Like Pearse a few years earlier, Connolly held that the leaders in Ireland had nearly always abandoned the people at the critical hour. Now crisis loomed and he was being told: "Bide your time". One day in January 1916 Connolly told an I.R.B. officer in Liberty Hall: "This 'bide your time' doctrine has ruined Ireland's chance of success before, and the same doctrine will ruin it now". However, the members of the Military Council convinced him that "the hour of the revolution" was near and this time would not strike in vain. They invited him to join them in planning for it and in its next edition *The Workers' Republic* carried the following statement:

> The issue is clear and we have done our part to clear it. Nothing we can say now can add point to the argument we have put before our readers in the past few months; nor shall we continue to labour the point.
>
> For the moment and the hour of the ripening, that fruitful blessed day of days, we are ready. Will it find you ready?

The hour of the ripening found the men of the Citizen Army ready. During the Rising, Connolly commanded all Republican forces in Dublin. He was wounded twice, the second time critically. After the surrender he was taken on a stretcher to Dublin Castle. A V.A.D. nurse describes the scene:

> The arrival of James Connolly caused an unusual stir. From the window I could see him lying on the stretcher, his hands crossed, his

head hidden from view by the archway. The stretcher was on the ground, and at either side stood three of his officers, dressed in the Volunteer uniform; a guard of about thirty soldiers stood around. The scene did not change for ten minutes or more; they were arranging where he should be brought and a small ward in the officers' quarters where he could be carefully guarded was decided upon. The nurses in charge of him acknowledged, without exception, that no one could have been more considerate, or have given less trouble. About a week after his arrival he had an operation on the leg. All through, his behaviour was that of an idealist.*

After the trial, Connolly smuggled his court statement to his daughter, Nora. In it he said:

> I do not wish to make any defence except against the charges of wanton cruelty to prisoners. These trifling allegations that have been made, if they record facts that really happened, deal only with the almost unavoidable incidents of a hurried uprising against long-established authority, and nowhere show evidence of set purpose to wantonly injure unarmed persons.
>
> We went out to break the connection between this country and the British Empire, and to establish an Irish Republic. We believe that the call we then issued to the people of Ireland was a nobler call, in a holier cause, than any call issued to them during this war, having any connection with the war. We succeeded in proving that Irishmen are ready to die endeavouring to win for Ireland those national rights which the British Government has been asking them to die to win for Belgium. As long as that remains the case, the cause of Irish freedom is safe.
>
> Believing that the British Government has no right in Ireland, never had any right in Ireland, and never can have any right in Ireland, the presence in any one generation, of even a respectable minority, ready to die to affirm that truth, makes that government forever a usurpation and a crime against human progress.
>
> I personally thank God that I have lived to see the day when thousands of Irish men and boys and hundreds of Irish women and girls were ready to affirm that truth, and to attest it with their lives, if need be.

Connolly was placed on a stretcher and taken to Kilmainham for execution. Since he could not stand they propped him in a chair for the firing squad. A Capuchin Father who attended asked the rebel leader if he would say a prayer for those about to shoot him: "I will say a prayer for all brave men who do their duty according to their lights", Connolly replied.

* Blackwood's Magazine, December 1916.

Roger Casement was the last to be executed in 1916. He was hanged at Pentonville Prison, London, on August 3, following trial and conviction under a medieval statute defining high treason outside the realm and written in Norman-French. His defence was that he was an Irishman.

He was arrested on Good Friday (April 21) near Banna Strand on the Kerry coast where he had landed from a German submarine. A few days later he was lodged in the Tower of London and held *incommunicado* under military guard until May 15, He knew nothing about the Easter Rising until it was all over and its leaders had been shot. He was aware, of course, that an insurrection had been planned.

Casement's prosecutor was the British Attorney-General, Sir F. E. Smith, two years earlier a fomenter of Tory rebellion against the crown in Ulster, later elevated to the Earldom of Birkenhead. If Smith's prosecution was vicious, Serjeant A. M. Sullivan's defence was inept. Sentence of death was pronounced on June 29 by the Lord Chief Justice, Viscount Reading, Smith's predecessor as Attorney-General.

The prisoner's speech from the dock was one of the finest of its kind, ranking with Emmet's masterpiece in the logic of its argument and the clarity of its thought. Casement laid bare the bankruptcy of British justice as applied to Ireland when he said:

> This is the condemnation of English rule, of English-made law, of English government in Ireland, that it dare not rest on the will of the Irish people, but exists in defiance of their will; that it is a rule derived not from right, but from conquest. But conquest, my lord, gives no title; and if it exists over the body it fails over the mind. It can exert no empire over men's reason and judgement and affections; and it is from this law of conquest that I appeal.

He noted too that "in Ireland alone in this twentieth century is loyalty held to be a crime". He spoke of the fate of those who had fought for the rights of the people, and of their failure. Then in ringing words he declared:

> Ireland has not failed. Ireland has outlived the failure of all her hopes. Ireland has seen her sons – aye, and her daughters too – suffer from generation to generation, always for the same cause, meeting always the same fate, and always at the hands of the same power. Still always a fresh generation has passed on to withstand the same oppression. For if English authority be omnipotent – a power, as Mr. Gladstone phrased it, that reaches to the very ends of the earth – Irish hope exceeds the dimensions of that power, excels its authority, and renews with each generation the claims of the last.

The cause that begets this indomitable persistency, the faculty of preserving through centuries of misery the remembrance of lost liberty this surely is the noblest cause ever man strove for, ever lived for, ever died for. If this be the cause I stand here today indicted for and convicted of sustaining, then I stand in a goodly company and a right noble succession.

Roger David Casement was 52 when he went to his death, a straight proud man to the very end. A large crowd outside the prison gates cheered when the bell tolled.

He had been in the British Colonial service for more than 20 years, ending a distinguished and humanitarian career broken in health. But his work had been for suffering humanity of the Upper Congo and the Putumayo* rather than the British crown, showing – as his Congo report put it – "what a hell on earth our own white race had made and was daily making, of the homes of the black people it was our duty to protect".

Casement did not come to Irish nationalism when he quit the colonial service; he had been a separatist for many years. In 1905 he wrote a friend: "The Congo question is very near my heart, but the Irish question is nearer ... It was only because I was an Irishman that I could understand *fully* the whole scheme of wrongdoing at work in the Congo".

He always returned to Ireland to rest after his wanderings in Africa and South America. In the early years of the century he supported Feis na nGleann in North Antrim and spent his holidays in the Gaeltacht. His friends – F. J. Bigger, Bulmer Hobson, Alice Milligan, P. S. O'Hegarty, Mrs. Alice Stopford Green, Séamus MacManus – were militant nationalists. He partly financed *The Republic* a journal published by the Dungannon Club in Belfast. And as an Ulster Protestant he organised other Ulster Protestants against Carson in 1913.

Casement was a leading member of the Volunteers. With Mrs. Stopford Green and Erskine Childers – Protestants all – he set up a committee to purchase arms in Germany. Childers landed the weapons at Howth on July 26, 1914, after a daring voyage in the yacht Asgard through treacherous seas and past British naval patrols. These were the guns that made 1916 possible.

When war broke and John Redmond declared for Britain, Casement was in America seeking funds for the Volunteers. From New York he wrote an "Open Letter to the Irish People" warning:

> Ireland has no blood to give to any land, to any cause but that of Ireland. Our duty as Christian people is to abstain from bloodshed; and our duty as Irishmen is to give our lives for Ireland.
> Ireland needs all her sons. In the space of sixty-eight years her population has fallen by far over four million souls, and in every

*In the Amazon Basin and claimed by both Colombia and Peru.

particular of national life she shows a steady decline of vitality....

Ireland has suffered at the hands of British administrators a more prolonged series of evils, deliberately inflicted, than any other community of civilised men. Today, when no margin of vital strength remains for vital tasks at home, when its fertile fields are reduced by set design to producing animals and not men, the remnant of our people are being urged to lay down their lives on foreign fields, in order that great and inordinately wealthy communities may grow greater and richer by the destruction of a rival's trade and industry. Had this war the highest moral aim in view, as its originators claim for it, it would still be the duty of Irishmen to stay out of it.

That statement was Casement's death warrant. He had declared war on the British Empire. From then on Whitehall used its immense resources to capture and kill him. He spent eighteen frustrating months in Germany seeking support for the Irish cause. He tried to form an Irish Brigade recruited from Irish prisoners of war; he had little success. He urged the Germans to send enough arms to Ireland to equip a nationwide insurrection; they sent the freighter Aud with 20,000 Russian rifles which finished at the bottom of the ocean. He travelled to Ireland by submarine with Robert Monteith, an I.R.B. man, and Daniel J. Bailey, a member of the Irish Brigade; the R.I.C. found him in a bush-covered ruin called McKenna's Fort about eight miles from Tralee the morning he landed and Bailey gave evidence against him.*

His enemies pursued Casement beyond the grave. Lest his execution damage the Allied cause, the legal adviser to the Cabinet, Sir Ernley Blackwell, recommended "by judicious means to use these diaries to prevent Casement attaining martyrdom". Basil Thomson, chief of the Special Branch, and Sir Reginald Hall, head of Naval Intelligence, had charge of the diaries. Details are still wrapt in mystery, but we do know that the British government in its "black propaganda" campaign mobilised King George V, Prime Minister Asquith, Ministers of the Crown, ambassadors, M.P.s, bishops, clergymen, journalists, poets, Whitehall clerks, Scotland Yard detectives. Even *The Times*, the voice of the Establishment, protested against the attempt to use the press to destroy Casement's character. But it had no sympathy for the dead man.

"It would have been fortunate for everyone concerned, and the simplest act of justice, if he had been shot out of hand on the Kerry coast", an editorial declared in a revealing phrase.

---

* Robert Monteith, a true man, escaped to America.

The View from Dublin Castle

The insurrection in Ireland, which broke out in Dublin on the 24th April, 1916, was the work of the Irish Volunteers, the Citizen Army and the Irish Republican Brotherhood.

Lt.-Col. Sir Matthew Nathan,
Undersecretary for Ireland.

PART TWO

For 700 years Dublin Castle was the seat of British government in Ireland. The Chief Secretary and Undersecretary had offices there. Also it housed the Attorney-General, the Solicitor-General, the Lord Chancellor, the Inspector-General of the Royal Irish Constabulary, the Chief Commissioner of the Dublin Metropolitan Police and the Commissioner of Prisons. The paraphernalia of government in Ireland had one function – the maintenance of "law and order". The seven centuries are marked by wars of conquest, famine, clearances.

Ireland was England's first colony. Before the Act of Union (1800) Dublin had an Ascendancy parliament which was abolished when it showed signs of independence. But Castle rule and the viceregal office continued so that in fact colonial status continued. By the start of the 20th century the office of viceroy (or Lord Lieutenant) had lost much of its power although the occupant continued to live in great splendour in the viceregal Lodge, Phoenix Park. The Chief Secretary, usually a member of the British cabinet, held the reins and made the decisions.

Augustine Birrell, a Liberal, was Chief Secretary of Ireland from 1907 to 1916. It seemed, when he took office, that the Irish at last had decided to accept British rule, as long as the hope of eventual self-government remained

"You may take my word for it", said Birrell, "that Ireland is at this moment in a more peaceful condition than she has been in, for the last 600 years". Birrell was a writer and sympathetic to Irish Home Rule aspirations. He travelled widely throughout the country. "I may have gone wrong one way or another", he said later. "but as far as knowledge is concerned, I believe I have more particular knowledge of certain portions of Irish life – not of all – than anybody has".

Yet it was during Augustine Birrell's tenure of office that the 1916 Rising took place. What he said about peaceful conditions was true, up to a point. One of his predecessors, the Conservative Arthur Balfour, who later headed a government, believed that British rule in Ireland could be enforced "by 20 years of resolute government" or by killing Home Rule "with kindness". From the 1890's on, the latter course was tried with some success.

Birrell listed the changes: "Self-government has been established in the counties on the most democratic plan with the most democratic results ever devised or accomplished, even by Tories, and though the experiment was a risky one, it has on the whole succeeded. The Irish Local Government Board though much exposed to criticism and coming in for a fair share of abuse, is essentially an Irish Board, and wholly outside what is called, often most uninstructedly, 'the Castle influence'. The Congested Districts Board, with enlarged statutory powers and a very considerable income, is also essentially an Irish Board, and within its powers, and within its income, supreme.

'The Department', as it is called, of Agriculture and Technical Instruction is Irish in all its ways, quarrels, and pursuits. And yet, despite these things, and in the face of prosperity among farmers, cottages for the labourers, and control over her most important affairs, no close observer of Ireland as a whole, during the last two years or so, could fail to notice that this Sinn Féin spirit was increasing".

The Chief Secretary overstated the gains; misery and poverty ahounded, especially in the towns and along the western seaboard (the Congested Districts), and the poor got scant justice. The seed of the "revolutionary madness" he noticed sprouting when the war began in 1914, had been in the ground a long time; generations of downtrodden people put it there. Birrell was nearer the truth when he said: "The spirit of what today is called Sinn Féin is mainly composed of the old hatred and distrust of the British connection, always noticeable in all classes and in all places, varying in degree and finding different ways of expression, but always *there*, as the background of Irish politics and character".

The Chief Secretary worked in London while Parliament sat. In his absence the administration of Ireland was run by the Under Secretary, a career official.

Sir Matthew Nathan, a former Governor of Hong Kong, was appointed in October, 1914. He was a cautious, quiet, methodical man. Reports came to the Castle by letter, telephone and cipher telegram. Every night Sir Matthew despatched a bag or two of papers to the Irish office at 37 and 38 Old Queen Street, London. He drew up reports of the state of Ireland for the Chief Secretary, who passed them on to the Government.

The Under Secretary had at his disposal the Royal Irish Constabulary, a paramilitary force established by Sir Robert Peel in 1814.* Its well-trained members were armed with carbines. They were all natives and knew the country and the people. Their primary purpose was to maintain British rule; they sniffed out sedition, stamped out rebellion and cleared recalcitrant tenants off their holdings.

Major Ivor Price, head of the Crimes Special Branch in Dublin Castle, and during the war, Director of Military Intelligence in Ireland, said of the R.I.C.: "As the Sinn Féiners themselves admitted, Ireland has been held by the police sergeant and his five men in each village. – ... The police all over the country have their eyes open and report upon everything, and it would be hopeless for the military to start an intelligence system without working through the police. There was absolute co-operation. I was daily at the Castle and saw the different members of the staff and the heads of the departments, and got all the information I wanted; and, if I made any inquiry, I sent to the police and they went on with the inquiry. I was in constant communication with London, and we would get information

---

* Peel's Peace Preservation Force became the Irish Constabulary in 1836 and after 1867 the Royal Irish Constabulary.

from there and sometimes from America, too, from American correspondents, then we would test the information we got here as well as we could".

No wonder Nathan told Birrell in a letter, dated December 18, 1915, that, in the event of a rebellion, "each policeman would be worth three soldiers". And the Chief Secretary in turn paid tribute to the thoroughness of R.I.C. reports: "... they enable anybody sitting either in Dublin or in London, to form a correct, general estimate of the feeling of the countryside in different localities".

Dublin was another matter.

Birrell admitted that the Castle was unable to get inside information on what the revolutionaries were planning in Dublin. The Dublin Metropolitan Police was unable to exercise the same surveillance in the capital as the R.I.C. in the provinces where every man knew his neighbour and could trace his family tree several generations.

The D.M.P. recruited in the provinces; they were big, brawny men and most of them saw Dublin for the first time when they entered the Depot. Of course, the D.M.P. Detective Department worked in close liaison with the Crimes Special Branch of the R.I.C.

Dublin Castle also had at its disposal, though not directly under its control, the military and naval forces of the Crown in Ireland; these took their orders from the War Office and the Admiralty in London respectively. As it turned out this was one serious weakness in the Imperial defences.

The Castle's extensive powers came from a variety of laws: the Explosive Substances Act; the Unlawful Drilling Act "to prevent the training of persons to the use of arms and to the practice of military evolutions"; the Criminal Law and Procedure Act (1887), which provided for special jury trials in proclaimed districts and empowered the Lord Lieutenant by proclamation to prohibit or suppress "dangerous associations"; the old Whiteboy Acts of the 18th and 19th centuries, which gave the Government power to deal with riotous or unlawful assemblies.

On August 8, 1914 – four days after the war began – the Defence of the Realm Act, 1914 (commonly called Dora) came into force to deal with "any manifestation of sedition or rebellion". In March, 1915, the Defence of the Realm Act Number Two granted rigbt to trial by jury – a serious weakness, said Castle officials.

When Under Secretary Nathan was asked by the Special Commission set up to inquire into the Rising why, with all its powers, Dublin Castle did not deal with the Volunteers, he replied: "We were not deterred from taking action by the absence of statutory powers; we were deterred practically for political reasons".

The Commission wanted to know who worked at Dublin Castle? Were the lower officials Irish or English? The great majority were Irish, Sir Matthew told the Commissioners.

Sir Malcolm Chambers, a member of the Commission, then put the following question: "May I ask you generally did you have loyal and efficient support from them?"

"Yes", Sir Matthew replied.

(2)

The most powerful force in shaping 1916 was the language revival movement, the non-political Gaelic League. It inspired Sinn Féin and later the Volunteers. It influenced life and literature by creating Irish-Ireland values with which the young could identify. It held a mirror up to the Gaelic past. Most of the makers of the Rising had been, in Pearse's phrase, "to school to the Gaelic League". It sparked James Connolly to write *Labour in Irish History* and *The Reconquest of Ireland*. From a tiny seed national resurgence grew.

The Gaelic League began modestly enough in a Dublin room on July 31, 1893. "A number of gentlemen have resolved themselves into a society for the sole purpose of keeping the Irish language *spoken* in Ireland", says the report of the meeting in the *Gaelic Journal*. Dr. Douglas Hyde supplied the idea. A keen student of the language, he noted sadly its tragic withering during the 19th century.

"At the time of the Great Famine in 1847-'48, it was the ordinary language of about four millions of people in Ireland", he wrote. "The Famine knocked the heart out of everything. After that it just wilted away until little more than three-quarters of a million, and the bulk of these aged people, knew anything about it ... Between 1861 and 1891 the language died out with such rapidity that the whole island contained, in 1891, according to the census, less Irish speakers than the small province of Connacht had done 30 years before – that was something over three-quarters of a million".

After the death of Parnell, a disillusioned young Ireland needed a noble cause and found it in the language. Opportunist politicians were degrading the country, spewing personal spleen from platforms in the name of Home Rule.

The old Fenian John O'Leary told the poet W. B. Yeats the politicians had "such low morals that they would lie, or publish private correspondence, if it might advance their cause". The young who joined the language movement contrasted the sordidness of the present with the glories of Gaelic civilisation. The great awakening began.

After 1905 Dublin Castle dubbed all Irish-Irelanders "Sinn Féiners". Many Gaelic Leaguers went into the new movement which Arthur Griffith, editor of *The United Irishman,* founded (Griffith's partner, William Rooney, was a language enthusiast). The paper ran from 1899 to 1906; Dublin Castle seized 23 issues. *Sinn Féin* succeeded it and ran to 1914 when it was suppressed. Like its predecessor, it fostered the language, nationality, Irish games and industrial development.

Griffith drafted Sinn Féin's political and economic doctrines. Grattan's Constitution of 1782 he believed to be the legal constitution of Ireland with its government of "King, Lords and Commons". He proposed setting up a council of 300 in Dublin, which Irish M.P.s would attend; the council, in effect, would become the Parliament of Ireland. He urged retention of the Crown link on the Austria-Hungarian model. Economically, Griffith derived his ideas from the German, Friedrich List. He wanted home industries fostered and protected, Irish savings invested in Ireland, shipping and waterways developed. These theories stimulated much discussion.

Sinn Féin's highpoint came in 1908 when C. J. Dolan, M.P. for Leitrim, resigned his seat and fought the by-election under the movement's banner and lost. By August, 1909, Sinn Féin had 115 branches. Dublin Castle reported a gain of 40 over the previous year.

In 1906 the Liberals swept to power in England with a majority so large they did not need the support of John Redmond's Irish Parliamentary Party. Three years later the House of Lords rejected Lloyd George's "people's budget" and the ensuing election gave Redmond the balance of power at Westminster. In 1911 he helped the Liberals pass the Parliament Bill ending the veto power of the Lords; the Upper House now could delay but not block legislation. The road appeared open for passage of the Home Rule Bill.

But the British Tory Establishment had no intention of permitting Home Rule. Even though control of finances, external affairs and defence would remain the prerogative of the Imperial Parliament, to them it spelt the break-up of the Empire. During the controversy surrounding the first Home Rule Bill in 1886, Lord Randolph Churchill had written to his friend Lord Justice Fitzgibbon: "I decided some time ago that if the GOM (Gladstone) went for Home Rule the Orange card would be the one to play. Please God it may turn out to be the ace of trumps and not the two".

As the third Home Rule Bill moved to its inevitable parliamentary triumph it was time to play the Orange card. Sir Edward Carson, a former Solicitor-General for Ireland, led the Unionist opposition. He aroused Protestant Ulster to the threat of Home Rule. With him stood the Conservative Party leader, Andrew Bonar Law, who declared, "We will support resistance to the end". The financial barons of England supplied the war treasury; Lord Astor gave £10,000; Lords Rothemere, Rothschild, Iveagh and the Duke of Bedford, £10,000 each; scores of others gave lesser sums. The Orange Order established the Ulster Volunteer Force, set up a shadow provisional government, purchased arms in Germany, landed them at Larne under the Nelson eye of the British Navy and threatened war on the Liberal Government of England.

Carson's aide, Captain James Craig (later Lord Craigavon), said he would rather be ruled by the Kaiser than by John Redmond. Brigadier-General Sir Hubert Gough, commanding British forces at the Curragh, and his officers said that if ordered to march on Ulster they would refuse. They went unpunished. That their attitude was shared by the top officers of the British

41

Army is clear from the following entry in the diary of Major-General (later Field Marshal) Sir Henry Wilson, then director of Military Operations at the War Office, under the date March 23, 1914: "Sir John French (Chief of the Imperial General Staff) sent for us at 1 o'clock ... Directly after all Commanders-in-Chief and Divisional Commanders came into the Chief of the Imperial General Staff's room and told us that the Army was unanimous in its determination not to fight Ulster. This was superb".

Carson, the man Scawen Blunt called a "Castle bloodhound", was a ruthless, able leader; he blocked Home Rule. Redmond, a good House of Commons man who believed in "imperial unity and strength" (his own words) as well as regional self-government for Ireland was unnerved by the Tory threats and lost the initiative. Under pressure from the Liberals, he agreed to partition "for a limited period". Carson rejected the "concession". Redmond momentarily fell back on the Irish Volunteers. When the war came Home Rule and Ireland's problems were put in cold storage for the duration. Carson joined the Cabinet* and Redmond urged his countrymen to go forth and die for the Empire.

(3)

In 1910, Sinn Féin announced it would not embarrass Redmond's campaign for Home Rule; from then until 1914 the movement faded away. It condemned partition outright.

"To even discuss the exclusion of Ulster or any portion of Ulster from a Home Rule measure is in itself traitorous", an editorial in *Sinn Féin* declared. It welcomed the Volunteers. "To help the Volunteer movement is a national duty: they may not defeat England, but the movement will help to make Ireland self-reliant". It stepped up its opposition to recruiting. (Dublin Castle had paid it the compliment in a 1907 report of saying the recruiting returns "showed a marked decrease as compared with previous years; this decrease counted from the commencement of Sinn Féin activity".)

Irish Freedom, for the Irish Republican Brotherhood, denounced the very idea of partition: "If this nation is to go down, let it go down gallantly as becomes its history, let it go down fighting, but let it not sink into the abjectness of carving a slice out of itself and handing it over to England".

The *Irish Worker,* for the Labour movement, declared: "To it (partition) Labour should give the bitterest opposition, against it Labour in Ulster should fight even to the death if necessary as our fathers fought before us".

Redmond, fearing the rising influence of the separatists and their policies, demanded that 25 of his nominees be placed on the Volun-

* He held office three times: Attorney-General of the first coalition, First Lord of the Admiralty, and a member of the War Cabinet.

teer executive; he wanted "tried and true" men, he said. Over the Opposition of the I.R.B., his ultimatum was accepted. The *Irish Worker* promptly attacked the new committee:

> Is there one reliable man at the head of the national Volunteer movement apart from Casement who, we believe, is in earnest and honest? ... We admit the bulk of the rank and file are men of principle and men who are out for liberty for all men; but why allow the foulest growth that ever cursed this land (the Hibernian Board of Erin) to control an organisation that might, if properly handled, accomplish great things?
>
> Our fathers died that we might be free men. Are we going to allow their sacrifice to be as naught? Or are we going to follow in their footsteps at the Rising of the Moon?

The *Irish Volunteer,* organ of the Volunteers, replied: "Force has re-appeared as a factor in Irish political life ... The object of the Volunteers is to maintain and preserve the right and liberties common to the whole people of Ireland. There is no question of preserving merely the 'legal' rights graciously permitted us by a foreign power .

(4)

As Europe marched to war in August, 1914, British Foreign Secretary Sir Edward Grey saw Ireland as "The one bright spot in the whole of this terrible situation ... The general feeling throughout Ireland and I would like this to be understood abroad does not make the Irish question a consideration which we feel we have now to take into account".

John Redmond agreed. "I was moved a great deal by that sentence in the speech of the Secretary of State for Foreign Affairs in which he said that the one bright spot in the situation was the changed feeling in Ireland', said Redmond. "In past times when this Empire has been engaged in these terrible enterprises, it is true – it would he the utmost affectation and folly on my part to deny it the sympathy of the Nationalists of Ireland, for reasons to be found, deep in the centuries of history, have been estranged from this country. Allow me to say that what has occurred in recent years has altered the situation completely ... And today I honestly believe that the democracy of Ireland will turn with utmost anxiety and sympathy to this country in every trial and every danger that may overtake it ...". He continued:

> Today there are in Ireland two large bodies of Volunteers. One of them sprang into existence in the North. Another has sprung into existence in the South. I say to the Government that they may tomorrow withdraw every one of their troops from Ireland; I say

that the coast of Ireland will be defended from foreign invasion by her armed sons, and for this purpose armed Nationalist Catholics in the South will be only too glad to join arms with the armed Protestant Ulstermen in the North. Is it too much to hope that out of this situation there may spring a result which will be good not merely for the Empire, but good for the future welfare and integrity of the Irish nation? I ought to apologise for having intervened; but, while Irishmen generally are in favour of peace, and would desire to save the democracy of this country from all the horrors of war, while we would make every possible sacrifice for that purpose, still, if the dire necessity is forced upon this country, we offer to the Government of the day that they may take their troops away, and that, if it is allowed to us, in comradeship with our brethren in the North, we will ourselves defend the coasts of our country.

Next day Britain declared war on Germany. Redmond had committed Ireland to her side, something which Keir Hardie refused to do on behalf of the British working class. Many Liberals opposed the Government; four Ministers resigned and Asquith feared a split. The eyes of Europe were on the Commons and Redmond's speech helped Britain greatly. Nor could the Irish leader have been under any illusion as to the nature of the war; for 10 years Britain had been preparing for it and the orders were all ready, as Connolly pointed out.

The war issue split the Volunteers. The original executive issued a statement on September 24 declaring that "Ireland cannot, with honour or safety, take part in foreign quarrels otherwise than through the free action of a National Government of her own". It rejected Redmond's claim to offer up "the blood and lives of the sons of Irish men and Irish women in the service of the British Empire".

Next day, Asquith and Redmond addressed a recruiting meeting in Dublin. On September 26, Redmond ordered his followers to form a new organisation called the National Volunteers; the Irish Volunteers were left with about 11,000 out of an enrolled membership of 180,000. Subsequently, according to Under-Secretary Nathan, about 30,000 National Volunteers joined the British Army.

"This was the moment of the greatest risk", said Chief Secretary Birrell. "Nobody could foretell what would happen in Ireland, or what her attitude would be. It might easily have demanded 60,000 soldiers to keep her down. Mr. Redmond's spontaneous, patriotic, courageous, but British speech was a bold stroke, and bravely has it succeeded. One hundred and fifty thousand Irish Volunteer soldiers are fighting, as Irish soldiers know how to fight, on the side of Great Britain. To me it is marvellous. But there were in Ireland men and women who thought that Mr. Redmond had thrown away a great opportunity and that he should have struck a bargain with the Crown ere he consented to become a recruiting officer for it. These men were in a small minority. Ireland preserved an unbroken front with the rest of the United Kingdom and the Empire and this she did to the bitter disappointment of Germany. But the minority were still there and were shortly to be increased in numbers".

The Irish Volunteers held a convention on October 25, 1914, under the presidency of Eoin Mac Néill and adopted the following declaration of policy:

1. To maintain the right and duty of the Irish nation henceforth to provide for its own defence by means of a permanent armed and trained Volunteer Force.

2. To unite the people of Ireland on the basis of Irish nationality and a common national interest; to maintain the integrity of the nation; and to resist with all our strength any measures tending to bring about or perpetuate disunion or the partition of our country.

3. To resist any attempt to force the men of Ireland into military service under any government until a free National Government of Ireland is empowered by the Irish people themselves to deal with it.

4. To secure the abolition of the system of governing Ireland through Dublin Castle and the British Military power, and the establishment of a National Government in its place.

Redmond's National Volunteers declined in numbers and influence. The War Office refused to recognise them despite their leader's earnest pleas; similarly his appeal that an Irish division with special insignia be organised was rejected.

"From the very first hour", he said in October, 1914, "our efforts were thwarted, ignored and snubbed. Everything almost that we asked for was refused and everything almost that we protested against was done". Yet his recruiting efforts did not falter.

But the campaign *against* recruiting took effect too. In the middle of 1915 the military authorities complained to the British Government that their efforts were being frustrated by "the hostile activities of the Sinn Féin supporters". Nathan consulted the Irish parliamentary leaders, Redmond, Joe Devlin and John Dillon. Redmond considered the separatists a negligible factor; Dillon thought them a danger.

Sir Morgan O'Connell of Kerry, kin of the Liberator, wrote to *The Times* about interference with a recruiting meeting in Killarney. He noted a change in the attitude of the people. He brought the Irish Guards band to the town, persuaded the P.P. to take the chair "and he made an excellent recruiting speech"; the chairman of the urban council "gave them a hearty welcome and everything went off splendidly". That was in May,

1915; later he couldn't get even a chairman for his meeting and the children of Kerry were singing "It's a Wrong Wrong Way to Tipperary".

According to Major Price, the anti-recruiting campaign cost the British Army 50,000 men. Lord Midleton was beside himself because of speeches in Cork by Father Michael O'Flanagan and Countess Markievicz; he demanded that the Castle lock them up. Birrell replied that to suppress the separatists "would probably result in shooting and divide the country during the war". He called Father O'Flanagan "a turbulent priest" and complained to his superiors. "Afterwards Father O'Flanagan explained to his parishioners from the altar that he would be silent".

The Bishop of Limerick, Dr. O'Dwyer, was in a different category. "He was very able", said Birrell, "although not a turbulent man". He wrote a stinging anti-recruiting pamphlet. The Bishop of Kerry, on the other hand, used his influence on the side of "law and order", according to Sir Morgan O'Connell.

The Castle began to note a change in the Irish priesthood. Their influence in rural areas was very marked, said Birrell. If they were strongly against Sinn Féin in a locality, the movement died. But some of the younger clergy had pro-Sinn Féin and anti-war views. The seditious press was also a menace; the papers were handed about from place to place. The Castle took action, but ways were found to outwit censorship and bans. As many as 50 or 60 persons read each copy. And teachers disseminated treason "through the medium of the Irish language".

Dublin was a hotbed of sedition; or so officialdom reckoned. Yet by 1916, when the Royal Commission sat, 17,536 had joined the British forces from the capital as compared with 11,568 from the rest of Leinster, 15,043 from Munster, 51,735 from Ulster, and only 3,920 from Connacht.

Nevertheless, the 2,225 Volunteers, armed with 825 rifles, and the nearly 200 Citizen Army, armed with 80 rifles, worried the Castle. (They had no worries about the 4,100 National Volunteers armed with 798 rifles). The I.R.B., "a small knot of violent men", as Nathan called them, had headquarters in Dublin. "These men worked with great secrecy", he continued, "never appearing on public platform or in the press, or making themselves in any way amenable to the law".

Then there was the Citizen Army. On November 26, 1913, Sir John Ross, Chief Commissioner of the Dublin Metropolitan Police, reported to the Government that the Dublin strikers were drilling. He wrote:

> I said it was the first occasion in my experience that organisations of a semi-military character had been formed in Dublin and I requested instructions before the movement became stronger. In reply I was directed to keep the matter under observation and to forward further reports. A few weeks later I bad again to write about this movement, saying that more men seemed to be enrolling and training themselves, that some of them carried hurleys – a wooden club used in a game which is not unlike hockey – and again I

repeated my first request. I added that the police had not observed any attempts made to carry firearms or sidearms. In reply, I got an answer similar to the one above referred to. I might just add here that Connolly, who was a prominent leader of this movement, said that they were arming themselves with these hurleys or clubs for the purpose of resisting the police, who were at the time put in the dock as it were.

The first time Sir John noted arms drilling in Dublin was on July 16, 1914, when his men reported seeing a number of Irish Volunteers training with four rifles. Ten days later the Howth gun-running occurred. Sir John was not on duty that Sunday. His assistant, Commander W. V. Harrel, got in touch wih a General Cuthbert at the Kildare Sreet Club and was advised to call out the military. The rifles landed from Erskine Childers's yacht were taken to safety – by Fianna boys with trek carts for the most part – but the King's Own Scottish Borderers fired on the people at Bachelors Walk. The inquiry into the killings led to the resignations of Harrel and Ross.

The Castle was unsure when the Citizen Army and the Irish Volunteers came together. When the Royal Commission sat after the Rising, Mr. Justice Shearman was equally puzzled. The following colloquy took place between him and Sir Matthew Nathan:

Mr. Justice Shearman – There is the Citizen Army and there is the Irish Volunteers as you call them, or as they call themselves. At some period or another they came together, but up to a certain time it is a fact, I rather gather from your report, that they used to manoeuvre separately? – Yes.

Were they ever seen together? – In the last few months we thought they were working together.

Do you know what brought them together? – They shared their dislike of England.

That they probably had for a very long time. You do not know any of the inner history and how they came to be acting under the one leadership? – How they came together, no.

All Nathan could say was: "It is believed that the close association between the Citizen Army and the Irish Volunteers dates only from the latter part of 1915, but there is no doubt that, in recent months, they worked under one direction, the Citizen Army leaders urging violent action on those of the Irish Volunteers".

It is to the credit of the men of the Citizen Army that the Castle knew so little about its "inner history". It wasn't for want of trying; sleuths followed them everywhere. Liberty Hall was under constant watch. On October 6, 1915, for example, the Castle noted that, at 12.45 a.m., 85 Citizen Army men carrying rifles marched from Liberty Hall to Werburgh Street under the command of James Connolly and Countess Markievicz. After manoeuvring in the vicinity of the Castle, they returned to Liberty Hall at 1.50 a.m.

On October 24, 1915, at 12.15 a.m., about 120 Citizen Army members, including 12 women and 20 Fianna boys, assembled at Liberty Hall. They marched to Christchurch Place under Connolly and the Countess. Eighty of the men carried rifles. The party divided into sections and manoeuvred in the neighbourhood of Francis Street and the Coombe. They were joined by 20 others with rifles and, at 3 a.m., left for Emmet Hall, Inchicore, where they took part in a dance being held there. At 5.20 a.m., 70 of the party left the hall and marched back to College Green where they dismissed at about 6 a.m. About 35 returned to Liberty Hall and broke off there, each man bringing his rifle to his home.

On December 5, 1915, at 12.15 a.m., 76 Citizen Army members – with rifles – assembled at Liberty Hall under James Connolly, Michael Mallin and Countess Markievicz. They marched to Cross Guns Bridge, where they broke up into sections – some going along Whitworth Road and others along the canal bank to Newcomen Bridge – and went through manoeuvres as they advanced. They returned to Liberty Hall at 3 a.m.

The Castle recorded Volunteer manoeuvres too. On February 5, 1916, between 10.30 p.m. and 11 p.m. about 350 Volunteers – 200 with rifles – assembled at Blackhall Place and engaged in manoeuvres which extended as far as Phoenix Park, North Circular Road, Kingsbridge and Thomas Street. The party on the south side returned to Blackhall Place at 1.30 a.m. and marched from there to 41 Rutland Place, where they disbanded at 2 a.m.

The Royal Commission summed up as follows:

> During the greater part of the period the Citizen Army remained distinct from the Irish Volunteers. The movement which led to the formation of the former body, composed chiefly of Dublin workmen, was to a large extent inspired by anarchist sentiment based on Irish discontent. The leader was James Connolly, who is described as a man of great energy and ability. By the month of November, 1915, it was known that the two bodies were acting in combination in Dublin.

In the newspaper *The Workers' Republic*, edited by James Connolly, the following passage occurs: "The Irish Citizen Army was the first publicly organised citizen force south of the Boyne. Its constitution pledged and still pledges its members to work for an Irish Republic and for the emancipation of Labour".

Throughout the whole of this year Ireland was in a state of great prosperity so that Irish discontent could hardly be attributed to economic conditions, except that the housing of the working classes in the city of Dublin might have accounted for an underlying sense of dissatisfaction with existing authority, the authorities believed.

Dublin Castle did not expect a rising. It believed it had the Irish situation well in hand. Its reasoning was as follows:

"Generally, a rising either in the country or in Dublin, except in support of any enemy that had landed, was looked upon as most improbable. Neither the strength, armament, nor training of the Volunteers was of a nature that seemed likely to promise to them a measure of success as would lead them to make the attempt".

Reports from the provinces were reassuring. "They are very loyal in Galway city", noted County Inspector G. B. Ruttledge. "They recruited very largely for the army. The town of Galway is not in sympathy with the Sinn Féin Volunteers at all or with the Sinn Féin movement".

Matters were different in the Athenry area. "There is always trouble there", said County Inspector E. M. Clayton. Secret societies had existed down the years "and the people were imbued with the revolutionary spirit of '67, '48, '98 days". The energetic young Liam Mellows was Volunteer organiser. During Land League days the area was the scene of "very many agrarian outrages", according to Clayton. "They became so expert with and accustomed to firearms that the teaching 'to rise with arms' did not shock them; they glided quietly into the new condition of affairs".

County Inspector H. O. H. Hill of Kerry reported: "The Sinn Féin movement first came into prominence in Kerry in October, 1914, after Mr. John Redmond had announced the decision of the Nationalist Party to support England in the war". Kerry volunteers rejected Redmond's policy at a meeting in Tralee on October 14, 1914. The organisers in the county were two northern Protestants, Ernest Blythe and Alfred Cotton. Hill found them very active men and told the Commission with some indignation: "They were both from the North. They were not Southerners at all. They worked hard and earned their pay".

County Inspector P. C. Power of Kilkenny noted that his troubles began when Seán Mac Diarmada and Liam Mellows – he called them "John MacDermott" and "William Mellows" – addressed meetings in the district. "At that time a good deal of seditious literature and leaflets and newspapers were in circulation". Who were the separatists in Kilkenny? "So far as I know", said Power, "the movement in our district was made up principally of labourers, shop boys, clerks and others of that description". No men of property.

It was the same in Clare, according to County Inspector Gelston. They were "small farmers and herds". O'Loughlin (the chief figure) "was only a small farmer".

Likewise in Cork, reported Chief Inspector Howe: " In March 1916, the Irish Volunteer membership was 653 in Cork, East Riding and City, at which it practically stood. It received no support from any influential persons from its inception up to the rebellion. It was principally composed of shop assistants, clerks, artisans, labourers, and, in country districts, of small farmers' sons as well".

The R.I.C. submitted a memorandum to Dublin Castle on Septemher 14, 1915, stating: "As already reported, according to the confidential information, at a meeting of the Council of the Irish Volunteers held in Dublin on 30th May, 1915, Professor Mac Néill in the chair, a resolution in favour of the Irish Volunteers declaring themselves in favour of immediate insurrection, proposed by Bulmer Hobson was defeated only by the casting vote of Professor Mac Néill".

On November 13, 1915, the R.I.C. sent the following to Dublin Castle: "According to information from a reliable source, the Sinn Féiners have already planned a rising in the event of conscription and as this is perhaps the one object in which they would find many Redmondites in agreement with them, they might give a serious amount of trouble".

On November 29: "As it is, in the event of an invasion, or of any serious reverse to our troops in the field, the Irish Volunteer Force would seriously embarrass arrangements for home defence".

Extract of letter from Under Secretary to Chief Secretary, December 18,1915:

> He (Redmond) knows or should know that the enrolled strength of the Sinn Féin Volunteers has increased by a couple of thousand active members in the last two months to a total of some 13,000 and each group of these is a centre of revolutionary propaganda. He knows, or should know, that efforts are being made to get arms for the support of this propaganda – that the Irish Volunteers have already some 2,000 rifles, that they have their eyes on the 10,000 in the hands of the supine National Volunteers, and that they are endeavouring to supplement their rifles with shotguns, revolvers and pistols ... Unless in other matters we keep these revolutionaries under observation, we shall not be in a position to deal with the outbreak, which we hope will not occur, but which undoubtedly will follow any attempt to enforce conscription, or, even if there is no such attempt, might take place as a result of continual unsuccess of the British arms.

On March 17, 1916, the Volunteers held parades throughout the provinces. Reporting that 4,500 turned out – 1,817 armed – the Inspector-General of the R.I.C., Sir Neville Chamberlain, remarked:

"There can be no doubt that the Irish Volunteer leaders are a pack of rebels who would proclaim their independence in the event of any favourable opportunity; but with their present resources and without substantial reinforcements it is difficult to imagine that they will make even a brief stand against a small body of troops. These observations, however, are made with reference to the provinces and not to the Dublin Metropolitan area, which is the centre of the movement".

The Castle noted towards the end of the same month a statement by the executive of the Volunteers that the movement "cannot submit to be disarmed, and that the raiding for arms and the attempted disarming of men, therefore, in the natural course of things can be met only by resistance and bloodshed".

Following meetings in Dublin on April 7 protesting against deportation orders, Col. Edgeworth-Johnstone, Chief Commissioner of the D.M.P., reported to the Castle: "The Sinn Féin party are gaining in numbers, in equipment, in discipline, and in confidence, and I think that drastic action should be taken to limit their activities. The longer this is postponed the more difficult it will be to carry out".

When the Under Secretary read the note on April 10 he wrote on it: "Chief Secretary and the Lord Lieutenant to see the Chief Commissioner's minute". The Chief Secreary read it on April 12 and scribbled underneath: "Requires careful consideration. Is it thought practicable to undertake a policy of disarmament, and, if so, within what limits, if any, can such a policy be circumscribed?" On the same day the Lord Lieutenant read the minute and wrote on it:

"This is a difficult point; could the disarming be satisfactorily effected?" No decision was taken.

On April 17 Dublin Castle learned indirectly that a ship had left Germany for Ireland on April 12, accompanied by two submarines. The message added that the ship was due to arrive on April 21 and that a Rising was timed for the eve of Easter. The report was accompanied by a caution as to its accuracy. It originated in an extraordinarily casual fashion. Two days earlier, General Stafford, General-Officer-Commanding Munster, wrote General Friend, General-Officer-Commanding British forces in Ireland, that the Naval Officer Commanding Queenstown had been informed by the Admiralty in London that a ship and submarine were on the way.

The Admiralty learned about it from Washington after U.S. secret service agents had raided a German office in New York. But the British placed little credence in the story and did not even bother to tell Dublin Castle directly. When Lord Wimborne, the Lord Lieutenant, was informed he was so sceptical that he got the story wrong; he thought the ship had left America for Ireland. He remarked later:

"This was the only warning other than the facts of general notoriety which came to my cognisance prior to the day of the Rising".

Lord Wimborne had been presing for more troops to be sent to Ireland and the internment of the revolutionary leaders; he also wanted to have Clarke, Connolly and others he didn't specify deported. Various conferences were held at the War Office on the subject of Ireland; mostly they discussed the difficulties of recruiting. At one of these Lord Wimborne told the Commander of the Home Forces, Lord French, that "what has always worried me is that we have not enough troops in Ireland in case of internal trouble". He seems to have been assured that they could get them over from England pretty fast should the need arise.

On the other hand, Major Price, the military intelligence chief, reported to the Castle on April 10 that "the general state of Ireland apart from recruiting and apart from the activities of the pro-German Sinn Féin minority, is thoroughly satisfactory. The mass of the people are sound and loyal as regards the war and the country is in a very prosperous state and free from ordinary crime". He thought the Volunteers would rebel "if ever they get a good opportunity", giving as an example a "hostile landing". He also forwarded a letter from a student at St. Mary's College, Dublin, to a friend in America; the letter had been intercepted. It was written in Irish but was translated for the Chief Secretary's benefit. It said in part:

> They (the Volunteers) are getting stronger every day. Many converts are being made, for it is known now that they are our only hope since they put down conscription some time ago. Redmond is done for. Whoever wins the war, this country will be wronged and plundered, but the people of Ireland are not disposed of yet. Their spirit is always improving and growing more Irish .. . One thing is clear in all this: an end is being put to the rule and insolence of the peelers; they are not nearly so arrogant as they used to be – I hope to God we may see you in Ireland when you have finished your time over there. We want the like of you to strike a strong blow at John Bull – Easter will be soon over, then there will be summer coming on, May and June will pass by, not very hot as yet, and then – ! You know as well as I do and no doubt much better.

The usual notations accompanied the letter as it moved up the ladder of authority. Under Secretary Nathan wrote: "The outbreak after the summer I look upon as mere talk". Chief Secretary Birrell wrote: "The whole thing is rubbish". Lord Wimborne initialled the document but made no comment.

(6)

Major-General L. B. Friend came to Ireland in January, 1913, to take charge of the administrative branch of the army. In September, 1914, he was named commander of the forces in Ireland. The country was vital to Britain strategically with its four major ports – Belfast, Lough Swilly, Berehaven and Queenstown – and the great military training centre at the Curragh, Co. Kildare.

In 1916, Brigadier-General Lowe commanded the Curragh and Col. Kennard commanded the troops in Dublin. The Dublin troops consisted of the 6th Cavalry at Marlborough Barracks, the 3rd Royal Irish Regiment at Richmond Barracks, the 3rd Royal Irish Rifles at Portobello Barracks, the 10th Royal Dublin Fusiliers at Kingsbridge. Dublin garrison strength was 120 officers and 2,265 other ranks.

In case of trouble the mobile column at the Curragh, 2,500-strong, could be despatched to any part of the country on the same day. The 25th Reserve Brigade was available in Belfast and a field Artillery regiment in Athlone.

General Friend had a capable staff. As well as Major Price, his intelligence director, he relied on Col. Cowan, military secretary of the Irish Command, and Major Owen Lewis, who was described by Lord Wimborne as "a very able soldier". They and their chief did not believe a rising was imminent; at worst, they felt a collision might occur between police and Volunteers or between military and Volunteers.

General Friend left for England on Thursday, April 20. He didn't bother to tell Dublin Castle of his plans, but, on Saturday morning he called to Home Forces headquarters in London, chatted to some of the officers, then left for the country to enjoy the Easter holiday weekend.

The events of Friday, April 21, changed the situation for Dublin Castle. It learned that three men had landed from a submarine in Kerry on the previous night and that one had been seized. At the same time the Admiralty signalled that a ship under convoy off Queenstown had been scuttled, and its crew of three officers and 19 seamen, all Germans, taken prisoner.

Next day, Under-Secretary Nathan told the Lord Lieutenant that the man captured in Kerry was Sir Roger Casement. They discussed the situation and agreed that the events of the previous day must have dismayed the rebel leaders. Wimborne learned too, that the *Irish Volunteer*, in its issue dated April 22, had carried the following notice:

> Arrangements are now near completion in all the more important Brigade areas for the holding of a very interesting series of manoeuvres at Easter. In some instances the arrangements contemplate a one or two-day bivouac. As for Easter, the Dublin programme may well stand as a model for other areas.

The *Sunday Independent* published MacNéill's order countermanding the manoeuvres. Nathan called at the Viceregal Lodge at 10.30 a.m., told Wimborne that a quantity of gelignite had been seized near the city during the night and that Liberty Hall was under surveillance. The Lord Lieutenant urged him to raid the hall and other Sinn Féin "arsenals" and to arrest the chiefs of the conspiracy.

Then Wimborne wrote to the Chief Secretary in London: "I have strongly urged him (Nathan) at the same time to put his hands on the ringleaders, who, having countermanded their Easter Day parade, are probably sitting in conclave conspiring against us. The evidence is now sufficient for any measure we think desirable. The whole of them could be arraigned for association with the King's enemies and there is our internment policy safely in port. I am afraid if we stir up the hornets' nest and leave the hornets that we may have serious trouble. This haul, if successful, even will not deprive them of all their ammunition.

"As for 'our friend' (Casement), what a stroke of luck and what credit to the police and executive. I hope there will be no nonsense about clemency. He must be made an example of. He expects nothing else, I understand. These fellows have enjoyed too much immunity already. After all, it is nothing else than to create a diversion in favour of the enemy and detain three or four divisions here to deal with it – at a critical moment too. I want to implicate as many of the Sinn Féiners as I can with the landing – invasion, in fact. It has changed everything and justified our altering our attitude. A public trial, if there are not bad difficulties in the way, would bring it home best. I fear they will deny here and in Berlin the identity of our prisoner. I will write you more coherently tomorrow. This is in great haste for the post. I hear there is still a possibility of conscription. All the more reason for getting our suspects packed away. We shall never get a better opportunity or justification. If you agree, do write and ginger Nathan. I have never made much of their movements, or have been or am now an alarmist, but if you don't take your chances they do not recur".

Nathan, Col. Cowan and Major Lewis held a conference with the Lord Lieutenant at 6 p.m. They discussed the proposed raid on Liberty Hall; the officers said they needed an artillery piece to effect an entry, that one could be brought up from Athlone but that there wasn't enough time to do the job that night. They had 400 men permanently under arms in Dublin. The Lord Lieutenant, who was due in Belfast, decided to stay in Dublin until the revolutionary leaders were under lock and key.

At 10 p.m. a larger group assembled at the Viceregal Lodge. Among the conferees were the Under-Secretary, the Chief Commissioner of the D.M.P., Col. Edgeworth-Johnstone; the Director of Military Intelligence, Major Price; Col. Cowan, Major Lewis and a Captain Robertson. Wimborne again urged an immediate round-up. Nathan demurred; he wanted to know what charge could be preferred? To take action on the grounds of "hostile association" required the concurrence of the Home Secretary, he said. The Lord Lieutenant takes up the story:

"I argued that the prisoners could be remanded until this concurrence was forthcoming. I offered to sign the warrants and take full responsibility for possible illegality. I next discussed with the Chief Commissioner the systematic disarmament by night visitation of the Irish Volunteers in Dublin for a future night. The Chief Commissioner said it was feasible and concurred. Agreed to press arrests policy and abandon Liberty Hall raid. On the conclusion of the conference I urged upon the Under-Secretary in the strongest possible language the need for immediate and vigorous action and offered to take all responsibility".

Major Price said some weeks later: "At the conference, the Lord Lieutenant, who perhaps did not realise things properly, was rather hasty and wanted to rush Liberty Hall for the purpose of getting back 250 lb. of dynamite brought in there the night before. The proposal was that 100 soldiers and 100 police should rush Liberty Hall, but those who knew that the Liberty Hall people had been manufacturing bombs at Kimmage, Larkfield, Croydon Park and other places, and that the leaders would not be in Liberty Hall, knew we would probably lose 100 lives in the attempt, then the press would come down upon us and say that no rising was ever intended and that it was another 'Bachelor's Walk' affair".

At 6 a.m. on Easter Monday, Under-Secretary Nathan learned that one of the men who travelled with Casement from Berlin, ex-British soldier prisoner-of-war, Daniel Julian Bailey, of the Irish Brigade, was in custody and had confessed. Bailey said a Rising was planned for Easter and the Castle would be attacked.

Some hours later Nathan headed for the Phoenix Park. After discussing the latest news with the Lord Lieutenant, Nathan read ciphers he was sending the Chief Secretary seeking permission to arrest the revolutionary leaders right away. However, Wimborne and Nathan agreed that a Rising was now unlikely. The time was 10 a.m.

When Nathan returned to the Castle he rang A. H. Norway, Secretary of the Post Office in Ireland, at the G.P.O., and called him over for a conference. At 11.45 Major Price dropped into the Under-Secretary's office. They discussed details of the proposed arrests and disarming of the Volunteers and Citizen Army. They agreed that the crisis was over.

"The countermanding of the order, and the knowledge that Casement was arrested and the ship sunk, made us think the whole thing was off", said Price. "Anybody would".

The clocks of Dublin rang noon. Minutes later Nathan and Price heard shooting nearby. "They have commenced", said the intelligence officer, and he dashed into the Castle Yard, drawing his revolver as he ran. At the main gate, 25 yards away, he saw armed men in green uniform and a policeman lying in a pool of blood. As the group broke up, Price started to fire.

The Lord Lieutenant was writing to Prime Minister Asquith deploring the delay in ordering the arrests of the revolutionary leaders when the telephone rang. It was a police message telling him the Castle had been attacked, the General Post Office seized, Stephen's Green occupied, nearby Ashtown railway bridge destroyed, and insurgents reported marching on the Viceregal Lodge itself. In utter amazement, Lord Wimborne glanced at his watch. The time was 12.30 p.m.

Later that afternoon the Lord Lieutenant wrote to Chief Secretary Birrell: "The worst has happened just when we thought it averted. The Post Office is seized – Nathan still besieged in the Castle, but I hope he will be out soon. Almost all wires cut. Everybody away on holiday".

The Fires of Easter

MAC DARA: *Give me a pike and I will follow Colm. Why did you let him go out with fifteen men only? You are fourscore on the mountain.*

DIARMAID: *We thought it a foolish thing for fourscore to go into battle against four thousand, or, maybe, forty thousand.*

MAC DARA: *And so it is a foolish thing. Do you want us to be wise?*

CUIMÍN: *This is strange talk.*

MAC DARA: *I will talk to you more strangely yet. (A cry is heard outside. One rushes in terror-stricken).*

NEWCOMER: *Young Colm has fallen at the Glen foot.*

MAC DARA: *The fifteen were too many. You should have kept all back but one. One man can free a people as one Man redeemed the world. I will take no pike. I will go into the battle with bare hands, (He passes out and the shout dies slowly away).*

The Singer by P. H. Pearse.

PART THREE

A few minutes after noon on Easter Monday, April 24, 1916, detachments of Volunteers and Citizen Army, totalling about 850 men, fanned out over Dublin. They wore uniforms, carried guns and marched openly. Their leaders issued orders. Few bystanders paid any attention.

Seán Connolly of the Citizen Army led his squad of 16 men, two girls and a boy, up Dame Street to the gates of Dublin Castle. They threw a home-made bomb, which failed to explode, shot the policeman on duty as he raised the alarm, seized the guard-room then withdrew under fire to the City Hall the rear of which overlooked the Castle Yard and many executive offices, including the Chief Secretary's suite and the *Evening Mail* and *Daily Express* building at the corner of Parliament Street and Cork Hill. The citadel of British rule lay at their mercy but they had not the forces to take it.

Ned Daly's men of the First Battalion took over the Four Courts, the great law buildings overlooking the Liffey, to guard the approaches from Phoenix Park along the quays. Thomas MacDonagh, with the Second Battalion, seized Jacob's factory in the heart of the old city. With a dozen men – later strengthened to 20 – young Seán Heuston garrisoned the Mendicity Institute near Usher's Island. Eamon de Valera, with the Third Battalion, moved into Boland's Mills by the Canal, next to Beggar's Bush Barracks, while one squad occupied Westland Row station, and another, houses on Pembroke Road, Haddington Road and Northumberland Road, near Mount Street Bridge, to cover the movement of British reinforcements from Dún Laoghaire (then Kingstown) port.

Eamonn Ceannt led the Fourth Battalion into the sprawling South Dublin Union; he set up outposts at Jameson's Distillery in Marrowbone Lane, Watkin's Brewery in Ardee Street (under Con Colbert), and Roe's Distillery in James's Street.

A Citizen Army contingent under Michael Mallin occupied St. Stephen's Green; they dug trenches, later found the position too exposed and moved into the College of Surgeons and other nearby houses on the west side of the park.

A column from Liberty Hall, with Pearse, Connolly and Plunkett in the front rank, swung out of Middle Abbey Street and rushed the General Post Office on Sackville (now O'Connell) Street. Among them was The O'Rahilly, Treasurer of the Volunteers, who loyally had supported his leader, Professor Mac Néill, in opposing the Rising. But when the die was cast he joined in with the comment: "I have helped to wind up the clock and must be there to hear it strike".

The Republicans cut rail, cable and telephone lines, but failed to seize the vital Crown Alley exchange. They set up barricades, fortified their positions, cleared lines of fire, sent snipers to the roofs, sentries to the streets and waited for the enemy.

The Rising was 24 hours late; the Military Council originally set Easter Sunday as the date. Professor Mac Néill, Chief of Staff of the Irish

Volunteers, and Bulmer Hobson, his chief aide, learned of the plan and arrived at The Hermitage on Thursday night to challenge Pearse. When Mac Néill heard what was afoot he is supposed to have said: "Short of informing the police I shall do everything in my power to prevent such madness". On Friday morning he drafted the countermand orders. Later in the day Pearse, Thomas MacDonagh and Seán MacDiarmada went to see him. After much discussion he agreed to resign as Chief of Staff; the I.R.B. seized Hobson and held him prisoner.

On Saturday, Mac Néill learned of the Aud's fate. Following a conference with The O'Rahilly, he sent couriers all over the country cancelling Sunday's mobilisation. That night personally he took the order to the editor of the *Sunday Independent* and inserted it as an advertisement. The Military Council met at Liberty Hall on Sunday morning; it was clear the Rising could not take place at noon. They decided to postpone it for 24 hours. Meanwhile, Thomas MacDonagh, as Commandant of the Dublin Brigade, drew up an order and despatched it to all Battalion 0/C's. It said:

> April 24, 1916.
> The four city battalions will parade for inspection and route march at 10 a.m. today. Commandants will arrange centres. Full arms and equipment and one day's rations.

On Monday at 9 a.m. the Military Council met again at Liberty Hall. The Dublin plan alone called for 3,000 men; there was no chance now that the rest of the country would rise. Nevertheless they decided to go ahead. They did not know how many would answer the call, but there was no division among the seven on the right thing to do. The Proclamation was ready.

Outside the G.P.O. on Monday at noon Pearse read the Proclamation, Connolly at his side. A small crowd listened. The words may have meant little to them but they did learn that "Ireland, through us, summons her children to her flag and strikes for her freedom". Later, those who wished could study it more carefully by reading the copies posted on the front of the Post Office:

> We declare the right of the people of Ireland to the ownership of Ireland, and to the unfettered control of Irish destinies, to be sovereign and indefeasible. The long usurpation of that right by a foreign people and government has not extinguished the right, nor can it ever be extinguished except by the destruction of the Irish people. In every generation the Irish people have asserted their right to national freedom and sovereignty; six times during the past three hundred years they have asserted it in arms. Standing on that fundamental right and again asserting it in arms in the face of the world, we hereby proclaim the Irish Republic as a Sovereign Independent State, and we pledge our lives and the lives of our

comrades-in-arms to the cause of its freedom, of its welfare, and of its exaltation among the nations.

The Irish Republic is entitled to, and hereby claims, the allegiance of every Irishman and Irishwoman. The Republic guarantees religious and civil liberty, equal rights and equal opportunities to all its citizens, and declares its resolve to pursue the happiness and prosperity of the whole nation and of all its parts, cherishing all the children of the nation equally, and oblivious of the differences carefully fostered by an alien government, which have divided a minority from the majority in the past....

The proclamation was signed on behalf of the Provisional Government by Thomas J. Clarke, Seán Mac Diarmada, P. H. Pearse, James Connolly, Thomas MacDonagh, Eamonn Ceannt and Joseph Plunkett. Pearse, as President, headed the Provisional Government; Connolly commanded the revolutionary forces in Dublin.

The G.P.O. served as general headquarters for the six days of the Rising. The Tricolour flew over it. When Connolly saw the flag flutter in the breeze he turned to onlookers to ask: "Isn't it grand?" Some agreed. The fast turn of events must have puzzled many. One man in the crowd offered the half-whispered, straight-from-the-heart comment: "At last!" He was Stephen MacKenna, scholar, journalist and poet. He stood around watching for five hours as the Volunteers erected sandbags, set up communications, drew in provisions, buttressed fortifications; then he offered his services to the new government. But Pearse knew he was an ill man, thanked him gratefully and sent him home.

It was spring. The sun shone. The leaves had turned green. The capital was in holiday mood; Fairyhouse racecourse was thronged. Weather-stained recruiting posters flapped from dead walls. Trams stood stalled at College Green. Off-duty soldiers and civilians huddled under the porticos of the Bank of Ireland; colonial troops on leave moved into Trinity College.

Rumours grew: the Germans had landed; the Turks had landed; Jim Larkin had landed with 50,000 Irish-Americans; the country was in arms. Nothing seemed too fantastic to be believed, save, perhaps, one utterly fantastic fact; that, for the first time in 700 years of British rule, Dublin was in the hands of the Irish.

Night fell. Except for sporadic shooting an eerie silence enveloped the city.

(2)

The British reacted quickly to the rising. Headquarters, Irish Command, learned of the rebellion – or riot, as they called it initially – at 12.10 p.m. The first train with reinforcements arrived from the Curragh at 4.15; they continued to arrive at 20 minute intervals until the mobile column of 2,500 men was concentrated in or near the capital. Troops in Belfast and England went on a "prepare to move" alert; some of the latter thought they were going to France. On Monday evening the Lord Lieutenant issued a proclamation:

> Whereas an attempt, instigated and designed by the foreign enemies of our King and country to incite rebellion in Ireland, and thus endanger the safety of the United Kingdom, has been made by a reckless though small body of men, who have been guilty of insurrectionary acts in the city of Dublin:
>
> Now we, Ivor Churchill, Baron Wimborne, Lord-Lieutenant-General, and Governor-General of Ireland, do hereby warn all His Majesty's subjects that the sternest measures are being and will be taken for the prompt suppression of the existing disturbances and the restoration of order.
>
> And we do hereby enjoin all loyal and law-abiding citizens to abstain from any acts of conduct which might interfere with the action of the Executive Government and, in particular, we warn all citizens of the danger of unnecessarily frequenting the streets or public places or of assembling in crowds.
>
> Wimborne.

On Monday night, under cover of darkness, the military mounted machine guns on the Shelbourne Hotel and, when day broke, enfiladed Mallin's trenches in the Green On Tuesday, Wimborne declared martial law. More reinforcements poured in; by noon the Castle was relieved and posts established between Kingsbridge, rail terminus for the South, and Trinity College.

Despite strong resistance, City Hall was taken; by then Seán Connolly was dead: he had been shot while raising the flag over the building on Monday. Citizen Army men entrenched in the *Evening Mail* and *Daily Express* building and in the Henry and James shop nearby were overwhelmed in a series of heavy bombing assaults.

Artillery pounded barricades at Phibsboro' and the military secured the North Circular Road. That was the limit of the counter-attack; other points held.

Republican morale remained high. An tOllamh Liam O Briain, then a student serving with the Citizen Army in St. Stephen's Green – although he was not a member of that force – sums up the mood of the revolutionaries: "Yet among us all was a vast elation. We seemed to breathe a purer air and dwell in sublime heights. It was a unique experience to feel that, once again, after a hundred years or more, the foreign yoke had been cast off, and that men in their own capital, with their own flag above them, should be standing at bay before the foe of their race".*

* *The Historic Rising of Easter Week*, 1916. (1923).

On Wednesday, the gunboat Helga moved up the Liffey to bombard Liberty Hall. The Loop Line bridge prevented direct firing; the shelling reduced the roof interior to rubble, but the walls of the building stood. Field artillery units trundled big guns to Tara Street; they wanted the street dug to form grips for the trails and tried to impress local labour for the work. Dublin workmen refused. Some Trinity students pitched in; an *Irish Times* reporter noted that after an hour's work only two cobblestones had been lifted at the cost of a broken crowbar.

They mounted machine-guns on the Custom House, Tara Street fire station, and the Tivoli music-hall (now the *Irish Press* building). Field pieces and machine-guns then opened up on the centre of Dublin. Heaviest hit was the Beresford Place-Gardiner Street area. But the effect on the main Republican positions in the O'Connell Street-Middle Abbey Street sector was slight.

The defenders of the Mendicity Institute had been without food or sleep from Monday while under incessant attack. Bombing parties broke through on Wednesday morning; British losses were heavy, but Heuston and his men were forced to surrender.

The South Dublin Union was also under continuous assault from the start. By Wednesday the British had occupied the southern part of the grounds and were advancing on the main building; they were hurled back. Cathal Brugha by himself held the building on Thursday after the others received a confusing "withdraw" order, at the cost of a score of bullets in his body. The enemy again withdrew and the defenders held out until Sunday morning.

Reinforcements from England arrived at Dún Laoghaire on Wednesday. They disembarked unopposed because the mobilisation of Volunteers in the Dún Laoghaire-Blackrock area had been a failure. The troops were raw; their officers had been told German agents were terrorising Dublin. They moved towards the city in two columns: one along the interior Stillorgan-Donnybrook road, the other along the coast road via Blackrock and Ballsbridge. The first reached the centre of Dublin without firing a shot; the second ran into the determined squad of men who covered Mount Street Bridge from Clanwilliam House, the Parochial Hall and 25 Northumberland Road; two men held the latter. The British mounted attack after attack and piled their dead along the canal. When at last they took the bridge, darkness had fallen and the badly shaken troops set up camp in Mount Street.

Bombardment of the city continued on Thursday. The incendiary shells started numerous fires; sheets of flame roared skywards. By day a pall of smoke hung over Dublin. By night the burning buildings illuminated the capital. The *Irish Times* reported:

> The Hotel Metropole and all that block of buildings for a long distance into Middle Abbey Street were burned down, including the *Freeman's Journal* and *Evening Telegraph* offices, Messrs. Easons,

Messrs. Mansfields, and Messrs. Thom's printing establishment. Then the General Post Office was given to the flames and was destroyed – only the bare walls of this fine building remain. This particular fire extended down Henry Street as far as the large warehouse of Messrs. Arnott & Co., which remained intact but was flooded with water. The Coliseum Theatre was also destroyed.

On the opposite side of Sackville Street all the shops were burned down from Hopkins's Corner, at O'Connell Bridge, right up to the Tramway Company's office, at Cathedral Street. The fire extended backwards and enveloped and destroyed almost all the houses between Eden Quay and Lower Abbey Street, down to Marlborough Street.

As the guns boomed and the fires raged, writer James Stephens walked through Dublin. They were days of brilliant sunshine. One day he met an old Ascendancy man up from the country. "I am an Irishman and I hate to see that being done to other Irishmen", the old man said as the shells whined overhead. Another time he talked with a worker who told him about the Citizen Army. "The men I know", said the labourer, "would not be afraid of anything and they are in the Post Office now". "What chance have they?" Stephens asked. "None", the man replied. "And they never said they had and they never thought they would have any".*

He also asked himself some questions: "Was the city for or against the Volunteers? Was it for the Volunteers and yet against the Rising? It is considered now (a day or two afterwards) that Dublin was entirely against the Volunteers but on the day of which I write no such certainty could be put forward".

On Thursday night, "I saw a red flare that crept to the sky and stole over it and remained there glaring; the smoke reached from the ground to the sky and I could see great red sparks go soaring to enormous heights; while always, in calm air, hour after hour there was the buzzing and rattling and thudding of guns and but for the guns, silence".

On Friday, the sun shone through the pall of smoke; there were "no newspapers, no bread, no milk, no news", wrote Stephens. At noon the new British commander-in-chief arrived; he was General Sir John Maxwell and his first act was to issue an order promising "the most vigorous measures against the rebels and their sympathisers. "If necessary I shall not hesitate to destroy all the buildings within any area occupied by the rebels", he declared.

"We arrived at 2 a.m. From the sea it looked as if the entire city of Dublin was in flames", he wrote his wife. "These infernal rebels have got a lot of rifles with, apparently, a fair supply of ammunition. Everything is hung up, no food or supplies of any sort can be got. It is not safe to walk into the town. Grafton Street and all the shop parts have to be cleared of these infernal fellows who have occupied a certain number of houses and

* *The Insurrection in Dublin.*

snipe anyone who passes".

Later, Maxwell reported to Lord Kitchener at the War Office: "I do not like the temper of the people; all reports tend to show that a general rising could easily occur if outside support is forthcoming".

Friday was a day of terror and death. In the North King Street-Church Street area near the Four Courts, where the South Staffords commanded by Lt-Colonel Taylor operated, at least 15 civilians were shot out of hand. Taylor dismissed the murders with the following explanation:

> The operations in the portion of King Street between Linenhall Street and Church Street were conducted under circumstances of the greatest difficulty and danger for the troops engaged, who were subject to severe fire, not only from behind several rebel barricades which had been constructed across King Street, and other barricades in Church Street and side streets, but from practically every house in that portion of King Street and other buildings overlooking it.
>
> Strong evidence of these difficulties and dangers is afforded by the fact that it took the troops from 10 a.m. on the 24th of April until 2 p.m. on the 29th of April to force their way along King Street from Linenhall to Church Street, a distance of some 150 yards only, and that the casualties sustained by the regiment (the great majority which occurred at this spot) numbered five officers (including two captains) wounded, 14 N.C.O.'s and men killed, and 28 wounded.

When the massacre charges came to light, Maxwell said: "Possibly some unfortunate incidents, which we should regret now, may have occurred". The troops might have seen 'red'. "It" (the rebellion) "was allowed to come into being among these people and could not be suppressed by kid-glove methods, where troops were so desperately opposed and attacked".

The cordon of steel tightened. From the G.P.O. the desperately wounded Connolly ended an order with the words: "Courage, boys, we are winning, and in the hour of our victory let us not forget the splendid women who have everywhere stood by us and cheered us on. Never had man or woman a grander cause, never was a cause more grandly served".

(3)

The mobilisation on Easter Monday was quite small. The majority of the Volunteers who mustered were members of the I.R.B. What manner of men were they?

Sam O'Reilly was one. He and his four brothers Kevin, Desmond, Thomas and Donal – turned out with their father, J. K. O'Reilly. Their home in the North Circular Road was a centre of I.R.B. activity. Callers on Sunday morning often included Seán Mac Diarmada, Harry Boland, John

MacBride and Arthur Griffith. They were Volunteers from the time of the Rotunda meeting. Young Sam saw his first action during the Howth gun-running. He was one of the raiders in August 1915 who seized 200 rifles at the North Wall; the British had consigned them to Redmond's Volunteers. They took the weapons to Swords, erased the serial numbers, dumped them.

He was in Mullingar working on the Midland Railway before the insurrection. During Holy Week he got an order to report to his I.R.B. Centre in Dublin. He went to Seán Tobin's house. The place was packed with rifles; the living room had the appearance of a command post. He was detailed to go to Kerry by lorry to bring some of the Aud arms to Dublin. The journey never took place.

On Easter Monday, Sam O'Reilly was with his unit, the First Battalion, under Ned Daly. They mobilised at Blackhall Place.

Another who was at Blackhall Place that morning was young Tommy Dunne, son of a Fenian who fled to the United States after the Phoenix Park Invincible assassinations in May, 1882. He was no more than a boy when he shouldered his Howth rifle on Easter Monday; hut he was steeped in a tradition which held it a just thing that a man should fight to free his country.

Ned Daly addressed what was left of his battalion in the Gaelic League Hall; one who did not answer the mobilisation was Tommy Dunne's company captain. But it was too late to worry about such matters. Daly mounted a rostrum and said in substance: "When you leave here you will be going out to fight for Ireland. We intend to fight before giving up our arms. And if any man feels he does not want to join in that fight, he will remain behind when we leave". Only three remained behind.

Tommy Dunne's squad took over some houses on North Brunswick Street and set up barriers on North King Street and Church Street. Shortly afterwards a British soldier came sauntering down the street and Tommy jumped him; they imprisoned him in the Father Mathew Hall, where he was joined by 34 others before the week was out.

Later Tommy went on patrol to the Richmond Hospital, saw no enemy activity, returned to Ned Daly and ran despatches for the rest of the day.

On Monday night, Sam O'Reilly was put in charge of a detail assigned to blow up the Midland Railway lines near the Broadstone station. They blew up the permanent way, seized a steam engine and placed it on the up-line to block all incoming trains. They destroyed the signal system and cut telegraph lines. The official report describes their work in the following fashion:

> During Monday night troops had been ordered over the line and the rebels, having become aware of the fact, took steps with the object of wrecking expected troop trains. An abortive effort to destroy a culvert near the Liffey junction was made, and during the early hours of the morning, the cattle special, proceeding in advance

of the troop train, was derailed and wrecked. On the same morning an engine in steam at the Broadstone was seized by the rebels, and placed on the up-line, and started, those in charge jumping as soon as the engine began to gather speed. This act would have resulted in disaster if the runaway locomotive had met a troop train coming in the opposite direction but fortunately it was thrown off the line at the Liffey junction points. In consequence of this derailment, the troop trains could not come into the city. All telegraph wires were cut and service from Dublin was completely suspended.

On Tuesday evening Sam's contingent was at the Phibsboro barricade when the British demolished it with 18 pounder shells. They managed to break out of the cordon by splitting up; some moved to North Dublin to join Tom Ashe; others, Sam among them, headed for the G.P.O.

When Ned Daly decided to seize the Broadstone he sent 20 men under Paddy Holohan to do the job; one of the party was Tommy Dunne. But they had to advance across open ground, came under heavy machine gun fire, and were forced to retire.

Jim Mooney had the favourite backed in the first race at Fairyhouse and was leaning on the rails cheering with the rest, watching his horse move to the front when he heard muttered snatches of conversation about the Volunteers rising in Dublin and immediately left for the city. He caught the last train before the lines were cut.

He was a Dublin man, born in Seville Place in the parish of St. Laurence O'Toole. He had gone to Wales at seven when his family emigrated, later returning to Celbridge, Co. Kildare. He was working in Milltown-Malbay, Co. Clare, when the volunteers began and joined; when the split came he stayed with the Irish Volunteers. Later he went to Dublin and was a member of G Company of the Second Battalion; his company commander was Dick McKee. When the Easter Sunday manoeuvres were cancelled he went to Greystones and, on his return, travelled to Fairyhouse.

Knots of people stood at corners as he moved from the Broadstone to the G.P.O. They would stop their conversation as he drew near. The streets were silent; there was no traffic. Near the post office he saw grim reminders of the Lancers' futile charge. He found the windows sandbagged, sentries posted at the doors. Someone told him his unit was in St. Stephen's Green.

Jim Mooney trudged across O'Connell Bridge, down Westmoreland Street, by the Bank of Ireland, up Grafton Street to St. Stephen's Green. He found the gates padlocked and Citizen Army men digging trenches. Someone told him to return to the G.P.O., which he did.

Back at the headquarters of the Irish Republic he sought someone in authority, told his story again, discovered that his company was in Jacob's factory, was ordered to go home, get his equipment and report back; he could join his own unit the next day. They gave him the password –

O'Donnell Abú – but when he got back the sentry, a native of Glasgow, could not understand him and would not let him in. Jim was worn out at this point and was nearly ready to call it a day when someone with more authority than the Glasgow man came along and let him in.

He stayed the rest of the week; it was not possible to move across the city next day to Jacob's factory and besides they needed as much help as possible in the G.P.O. He spent the week on the roof of the building or fighting the flames. He was one of the group with The O'Rahilly during the final hours at Moore Lane. When they surrendered a wounded British officer paid them a compliment. "I wish I had a thousand of you fellows in France", he said.

Joe Clarke joined the Volunteers on the day after the Howth gun running. He was a member of the Third Battalion. They did foot drill on a vacant lot at the rear of Camden Row and practised miniature rifle firing. He mobilised at Earlsfort Terrace at noon on Easter Monday. About half of his unit – "C" Company – turned out. Lieut. Michael Malone marched them off to Mount Street Bridge; he put seven Volunteers in Clanwilliam House, four – including Joe Clarke – in St. Stephen's Parochial Hall just over the bridge and himself and one other took over 25 Northumberland Road.

They did nothing on Monday and Tuesday except look out the windows to see what was happening. It seemed to them that nothing was happening. They heard sporadic gunfire. Then, shortly after noon on Wednesday, they sighted the khaki-clad reinforcements from England moving towards them from Ballsbridge. The Volunteers opened fire as they drew near. The troops dashed for cover – right into the line of fire from Clanwilliam House. In a matter of minutes the leading British battalion was disorganised as the merciless crossfire caught the fleeing soldiers.

"We could see them crawling from garden to garden", says Joe Clarke. "There was little cover. We saw them dropping. The bodies were lying about the street".

The four men in the Parochial Hall had only 50 rounds each. Although the main British fire was directed first at 25 Northumberland Road and then at Clanwilliam House, the four kept blazing away whenever they saw a target until their ammunition was spent. It was 7 o'clock by then.

Bombing parties had stormed No. 25; Michael Malone died as the soldiers closed in; his comrade hid in the cellar and escaped. The four in the Parochial Hall hoped to get away under cover of darkness and reach another unit. They split up. Two were caught in a nearby house; Joe Clarke got to Percy Place before capture. He was lucky; a soldier fired at him but missed; the bullet went through a doorway. Inside the house a doctor was tending British wounded.

"He came out and wanted to know who was firing through the door", says Joe. "So they did not do anything to me; they just tied my hands behind my back with a pull-through and marched me off to Ladd Lane police station".

The fight was over for Joe Clarke but not for the little garrison in Clanwilliam House. With all opposition south of the bridge cleared, the British reorganised and moved up a second battalion. Crouching by the houses and gardens and stone steps, they dashed forward under heavy covering fire; each charge brought them nearer the bridge; each charge added to their casualties. But time and numbers told. Clanwilliam House was ablaze, its 0/C dead; the four survivors pulled out minutes ahead of the bombing parties that finally took the building.

The stories of these four citizen-soldiers may help one understand the kind of men who rose in 1916. None considered himself a hero, but all were heroes. There were fewer than 900 of them and they challenged an empire. They were ordinary men and their military training was minimal. In that lies their glory. They believed that Ireland should be free. In that lies their greatness.

Heavy fighting occurred in the North King Street area on Tuesday night. The British used prisoners as cover to cross the barricades; but the Volunteers held them at bay and succeeded in doing so for the rest of the week. They knew nothing about the surrender at the G.P.O. until a British officer shouted the information. Naturally, they did not believe him. Later Father Albert of Church Street confirmed the news; it produced a great deal of grumbling.

The surrender at Moore Street, where Sam O'Reilly was, did not win general acceptance, either. Some Volunteers had tears in their eyes; others were sullen.But Seán Mac Diarmada re-assured them; he explained why the decision was necessary, ending with the remark:

"This week of Easter will be remembered and your works will tell some day".

(4)

On Thursday night, Pearse reviewed the struggle for the benefit of his followers; it was like a "State of the Republic" message. There was much optimism in what he said, much prophecy, too:

"The forces of the Irish Republic, which was proclaimed in Dublin on Easter Monday, 24th April, have been in possession of the central part of the capital since 12 noon on that day. Up to yesterday afternoon the Headquarters was in touch with all the main outlying positions, and despite furious and almost continuous assaults by the British forces all these positions were then still being held and the Commandants in charge were confident of their ability to hold them for a long time.

"During the course of yesterday afternoon and evening, the enemy succeeded in cutting our communications with our other positions in the city and headquarters is today isolated.

"The enemy has burnt down whole blocks of houses, apparently with the object of giving themselves a clear field for the play of artillery and field guns against us. We have been bombarded during the evening and night by shrapnel and machine-gun fire, but without material damage to our position, which is of great strength.

"We are busy completing arrangements for the final defence of headquarters and are determined to hold it while the buildings last.

"I desire now, lest I may not have an opportunity later, to pay homage to the gallantry of the soldiers of Irish freedom who have during the past four days been writing with fire and steel the most glorious chapter in the later history of Ireland. Justice can never be done to their heroism, to their discipline, to their gay and unconquerable spirit in the midst of peril and death.

"Let me, who have led them into this, speak in my own name, and in my fellow-Commandants' names, and in the name of Ireland present and to come, their praise, and ask those who come after them to remember them.

"For four days they have fought and toiled, almost without cessation, almost without sleep, and in the intervals of fighting they have sung songs of the freedom of Ireland. No man has complained, no man has asked 'why?' Each individual has spent himself, happy to pour out his strength for Ireland and for freedom. If they do not win this fight, they will at least deserve to win it. But win it they will although they may win it in death. Already they have done a great thing. They have redeemed Dublin from many shames and made her name splendid among the names of cities.

"If I were to mention the names of individuals, my list would be a long one.

"I will name only that of Commandant-General James Connolly, commanding the Dublin Division. He lies wounded but is still the guiding brain of our resistance.

"If we accomplish no more than we have accomplished, I am satisfied. I am satisfied that we have saved Ireland's honour. I am satisfied that we should have accomplished more, that we should have accomplished the task of enthroning. as well as proclaiming the Irish Republic as a Sovereign State, had our arrangements for a simultaneous Rising of the whole country, with a combined plan as sound as the Dublin plan has proved to be, been allowed to go through on Easter Sunday. Of the fatal countermanding order which prevented those plans being carried out, I shall not speak further. Both Eoin Mac Néill and we have acted in the best interests of Ireland.

"For my part, as to anything I have done in this, I am not afraid to face the judgement of God or the judgement of posterity."

By Friday night the G.P.O. was a raging inferno. The weary defenders decided on evacuation. A van, dragged across Henry Street, screened them for the dash from the building. A young lad guarded Connolly with his body. The area was under heavy fire. Pearse was the last to leave; he checked first to ensure no one was left behind. The members of the

Provisional Government took up quarters in a house off Moore Lane. They had 17 wounded with them, including Connolly, who suffered great pain but remained in good spirits.

"Around us we could hear the roar of burning buildings, machine-guns played on the houses, and at intervals what seemed to be hand grenades", Nurse Elizabeth O'Farrell later wrote. During a sortie in Moore Street, The O'Rahilly was wounded; he died next day.

All through the night they tried burrowing from house to house towards the top of Moore Street. On Saturday morning the members of the Provisional Government held a council of war beside Connolly's stretcher in 16 Moore Street; they decided to surrender.

Seán Mac Diarmada gave Nurse O'Farrell a white flag; she moved up Moore Street towards the British lines and gave her message to the first officer she met. They escorted her to the Parnell monument where she saw Brigadier-General Lowe. He demanded unconditional surrender and gave her a half-hour to return with Pearse's answer. The Provisional Government sent her a second time to Lowe with a written message.

"Whatever was in the note from Commandant Pearse to General Lowe I cannot say", Nurse O'Farrell wrote. "But General Lowe's reply to it was: 'Go back and tell Mr. Pearse that I will not treat at all unless he surrenders unconditionally and that Mr. Connolly follows on a stretcher'. He told me then that unless Mr. Pearse and I came back in half-an-hour he would begin hostilities again. I brought back that message. The members of the Provisional Government having held a short council, Commandant Pearse decided to accompany me back to General Lowe."

The surrender of the fighting forces of the Irish Republic followed. Nurse O'Farrell went from garrison to garrison with the order from Pearse. It stated: "In order to prevent the further slaughter of Dublin citizens, and in the hope of saving the lives of our followers now surrounded and hopelessly outnumbered, the members of the Provisional Government present at Headquarters have agreed to an unconditional surrender, and the Commandants of the various districts in the city and country will order their commands to lay down arms."

Connolly counter-signed it with the comment: "I agree to these conditions for the men only under my command in the Moore Street district and then for the men in the Stephen's Green Command". MacDonagh held a conference with Ceannt, then added this note to the document: "On consultation with Commandant Ceannt and other officers, I have decided to agree to unconditional surrender also".

The cease-fire went into effect at about 4 o'clock on Saturday afternoon, April 29, although some posts on the south side did not receive word of the surrender until much later.

"The outcry among the men was frenzied", Liam O Briain notes. "It needed all the efforts of officers to prevent the wilder spirits from rushing out and seeking death in a last onset in the streets".

Thus ended the 1916 Rising.

Outside of Dublin, the country was quiet during Easter Week. There was some sharp fighting in north Co. Dublin under Thomas Ashe, some skirmishes in Co. Gaiway under Liam Mellows and a rising of local Volunteers in Enniscorthy. But that was all.

Ashe commanded the Fifth Battalion of the Dublin Brigade, sometimes called the Fingal Battalion. Each of the 48 men who answered his call had a bicycle as well as a rifle. They formed a mobile column and their tactics fore-shadowed the guerilla warfare of the Black and Tan years. They seized four police barracks and defeated a large R.I.C. relief force at Rath Cross, Ashbourne.

Mellows had plenty of men in Galway but few arms. He said later: "We had hardly any guns or ammunition. I had to send many of them home. I never knew the blackness of despair until then". They attacked a number of barracks, cut rail and telegraph lines, ambushed a reconnaissance convoy at Oranmore Cross, six miles from Gaiway, and almost panicked the garrison when word spread that they were marching on the city.

A sloop in the bay shelled the hills. On Thursday, the cruiser Gloucester put into Galway and landed troops. Mellows wanted to continue the fight after the surrender in Dublin but was over-ruled. The men returned to their homes, their leader went on the run.

Like the O'Reilly family in Dublin, the entire Fleming family rose in Clarinbridge, Co. Gaiway, under Liam Mellows. Michael Fleming, senior, was 49 years of age. Four sons joined him in the fight; Patrick, George, Michael and Joe. His eldest son Tom would have been there too but he was held up in Galway city. Three of the sons were interned in Frongoch after the Rising; the fourth, Michael, was sentenced to 12 months with hard labour. Michael Fleming, senior, was sentenced to five years. Both father and son were in the same prison – Lewes. The *Catholic Bulletin* reported in August, 1917, that when Michael Jr. was about to be released on expiration of his sentence, the father sought the Governor's permission to speak to him. "What!" said the Governor, "you have a son here!" "I have", replied Fleming, "and he would not he my son if he weren't here."

Michael Fleming, senior, was a fluent Irish speaker who "was always in the best of spirits, and extremely popular with his comrades". the *Catholic Bulletin* reported.*

The youngest son, John, who was about 16 at the time, ran messages for the Volunteers in Co. Galway during the Rising.

---

*His granddaughter, Mrs. Lulu Earley, has a small prayer book of his with the names of all the Lewes prisoners to prove his popularity. It is a valuable record.

Mr. Justice Shearman, during the Royal Commission sittings, asked County Inspector Clayton: "What has happened to Mellows?" He was told: "Mellows is on the run, too, with a good many more". Major Price assured the commissioners: "He is somewhere in Ireland. I hope we shall see him some day".

But they never found him. He escaped to America aboard a tramp steamer from Liverpool five months after the Rising. It took three months to complete the voyage. He returned to Ireland during the Black and Tan terror, and was executed on December 8, 1922, by the Free State Government after being held in Mountjoy Prison five months without trial.

(6)

All the "respectable" forces in Irish life condemned the Rising. John Redmond spoke for them. "My first feeling, of course, on hearing of this insane movement, was one of horror, discouragement, almost despair", he said. "I asked myself whether Ireland, as so often before in her tragic history, was to dash the cup of liberty from her lips; was the insanity of a small section of her people once again to turn all her marvellous victories of the last few years into irreparable defeat, and to send her back, on the very eve of her final recognition as a free nation, into another long night of slavery, incalculable suffering, weary and uncertain struggle". He went on:

> That doctrine has been contested only by the very same men who today have tried to make Ireland the cat's paw of Germany. In all our long and successful struggle to obtain Home Rule we have been thwarted and opposed by that same section. We have won Home Rule, not through them, but in spite of them. This wicked move of theirs was their last blow at Home Rule. It was not half as much treason to the cause of the Allies as treason to the cause of Home Rule.
>
> This attempted deadly blow at Home Rule ... is made the more wicked and the more insolent by this fact – that Germany plotted it, Germany organised it, Germany paid for it. So far as Germany's share in it is concerned, it is a German invasion of Ireland, as brutal, as selfish, as cynical as Germany's invasion of Belgium. Blood has been shed and, if Ireland has not been reduced to the same horrors as Belgium, with her starving people, her massacred priests, her violated convents, it is not the fault of Germany ...
>
> As to the final result. I do not believe that this wicked and insane movement will achieve its ends. The German plot has failed. The majority of the people of Ireland retain their calmness, fortitude and unity. They abhor this attack on their interests, their rights, their

hopes, their principles. Home Rule has not been destroyed; it remains indestructible.

Many local bodies followed Redmond's lead in condemning the Rising. British propaganda picked up their resolutions, distributed them widely in America and the Dominions. One county council said:

"We rejoice that this dastardly attempt has failed and that the people of Ireland have shown by their conduct in this crisis that Ireland is determined that her word shall be faithfully kept".

The remark is fairly typical.

The Council of the Cork Employers' Association viewed "with indignation and horror the shameful outrages which have been committed in Dublin and certain other parts of Ireland by a misguided and irresponsible section of the community, unable to distinguish between liberty and licence, and without any conceivable grievance whatever. The Council desire to humbly convey to his Most Gracious Majesty the King the expression of their unfailing loyalty".

The Dublin Chamber of Commerce thanked the army and navy authorities for their "prompt and successful action" in suppressing the Rising; they regretted that so many officers and men were killed and wounded in the fray. Some Irish groups in Britain, the U.S., Canada, Australia and South Africa also joined the chorus of condemnation.

Mr. John Sibthrone, chairman of the Council of Dublin Employers' Federation, went before the Royal Commission and blamed it all on the Dublin working class. "The Citizen Army was out for revolution", he said.

Mr. William Martin Murphy sent a memorandum to the Royal Commission. He put the whole trouble down to the 1913 strike: "It has been said so often, and it is so obvious that it is hardly necessary for me to repeat it, that the entire cause of this rebellion was permitting any people, no matter what their object, to be armed and drilled, and to possess arsenals unless they belonged to the regular forces of the Crown. If there were no organised armed men in the country, there could have been no attempt at rebellion".

The Archbishop of Cashel, Dr. Harty, on May 7, 1916 told a large congregation at St. Michael's Church, Tipperary: "We all know that the people of Ireland at large do not want any revolutionary measures". He continued: "We are perfectly well aware that the people of Ireland believe that by constitutional means they can obtain substantial redress of their grievances. The history of the past has shown that all revolutionary measures are doomed to failure. The people of this Archdiocese and of this town of Tipperary realise that to the fullest extent, and hence during the last sorrowful fortnight they kept calm, and showed that now, as always, they are true, patriotic Irishmen".

Dr. O'Dwyer of Limerick and Dr. Fogarty of Killaloe did not follow the lead of their metropolitan; the former denounced Maxwell in an "open letter" while the latter said that whatever the faults of the young men who rose in Dublin, they died bravely and unselfishly for what they foolishly believed was the cause of Ireland. They were lone voices for a time. But to the common people from the start, Pearse and his comrades were heroes like Tone and Emmet.

(7)

The British Cabinet decided on May 6 that Maxwell should be given a free hand on the matter of executions with these provisos: that no woman should be shot (Countess Markievicz was on the list) and that "death should not be inflicted except on ringleaders and proved murderers". Lord Wimborne thought the executions had already gone too far. Birrell and Nathan were relieved of their posts.

Prime Minister Asquith came to Dublin on May 11 and stayed a week. The murder of Sheehy-Skeffington disturbed him somewhat. But he explained it away with the comment: "On the whole except the Skeffington case there have been fewer bad blunders than one might have expected with the soldiery for a whole week in exclusive charge".

Sheefy-Skeffington was a Socialist and a pacifist. He was arrested in 1915 for speaking against recruiting and sentenced to six months' imprisonment. He went on hunger strike and was released. Before the Rising he wrote a letter to the *New Statesman* condemning British militarism in Ireland; it was not published until after his death. He also wrote an open letter to his friend Thomas MacDonagh, appealing to him to choose passive resistance rather than physical force in the struggle that lay ahead.

When the Rising came he organised a peace patrol to stop looting. He was returning home on Easter Tuesday evening when he was arrested at Portobello Bridge and lodged in Portobello Barracks; at midnight Captain Bowen-Colthurst took Sheehy-Skeffington as a hostage on a raid, brought him back to the barracks and, at 10 o'clock next morning, ordered him shot dead; two others – loyalist journalists as it turned out – were murdered at the same time.

That was one case; there were others. Mrs. Thomas Hickey of 170 North King Street told an inquest what she saw when she returned to her home on Saturday, April 29:

"When I rushed into the room, there I saw my darling son. He was lying on the ground, his face darkened, and his two hands raised above his head as if in silent supplication. I kissed him and put his little cap under his head, and settled his hands for death. Then I turned, and in another place I saw poor Tom (her husband) lying on the ground. 'Oh Jesus', I cried. 'My poor husband too'. And not far off lay the corpse of poor Connolly. I reeled round and remembered no more, as the soldier hustled me down the stairs and into the street".

Asquith visited Cork and Belfast; he met the leaders of the Unionist party. He believed they were ready to accept a partitioned Ireland with Home Rule for the South. He saw a chance for a deal between Redmond and Carson and he recommended Lloyd George for the Chief Secretaryship. The deal with Redmond and Carson called for partition during the war, an Imperial Conference afterwards. Lloyd George wrote his famous secret note on permanent partition and went on to the Premiership*

But that was some months ahead. Meantime, Asquith returned to London on May 19 and thought about Ireland. He "was inclined to put much of the Rebellion down to economic conditions", he told a friend, Lady Scott. "Some 12,000 families in Dublin live in single rooms". A few months later he was out of office.

(8)

The armed struggle was renewed in 1919 and continued until the Truce in July, 1921. In January, 1919, Dáil Éireann met and reaffirmed the Republic. In 1920 the British Parliament passed an Act partitioning Ireland and establishing parliaments for "Southern Ireland" (Twenty-Six Counties) and "Northern Ireland" (Six Counties). The Northern Parliament started to function in May, 1921, and, following the Treaty of December, 1921, a Southern Parliament took over in the Twenty-Six Counties, thus completing the partition of Ireland.

Accordingly, the promise of the Easter Rising, as enunciated in the Proclamation, remains unfulfilled.

*"My dear Carson – I enclose Greer's draft propositions. We must make it clear that at the end of the provisional period Ulster does not, whether she wills it or not, merge with the rest of Ireland."

Sir Francis Greer was parliamentary draftsman at the Irish Office. The letter was dated May 29th, 1916.

Arna chlóbhualadh in Éirinn ag Ardiff-Mahon, Baile Átha Cliath.